My Last Breath

J.P. LaRue

authorHOUSE®

AuthorHouse™
1663 Liberty Drive, Suite 200
Bloomington, IN 47403
www.authorhouse.com
Phone: 1-800-839-8640

First published by AuthorHouse 1/14/2009

ISBN: 978-1-4389-3003-9 (sc)
ISBN: 978-1-4389-3004-6 (hc)

Printed in the United States of America
Bloomington, Indiana

This book is printed on acid-free paper.

I dedicate this book to all the people who have helped me over the years

Prologue

Every man dies. For that is the nature of mortal man. We are all owed a death. I was seventeen years old when death found me, and my life was changed forever. I do not claim to have the answers. I can only tell you, the reader, what I went through and hope it helps in some way. Now, most of you reading this no doubt have seen movies and TV shows where people died, and were supposedly brought back after seeing a bright light. I don't doubt the validity of those claims. I think each person's death is different, just as each experience changes the person having it. I will try to tell you who are reading this what I saw and felt during that time after taking my last breath, and what followed after. My name is Josh LaRue and here is my story.

International Morse Code

Letter	Code	Letter	Code	Num	Code	Symbol	Code	Name
A	• —	N	— •	1	• — — — —	Ń	— — • — —	N with tilde
B	— • • •	O	— — —	2	• • — — —	Ö	— — — •	O with umlaut
C	— • — •	P	• — — •	3	• • • — —	Ü	• • — —	U with umlaut
D	— • •	Q	— — • —	4	• • • • —	,	— — • • — —	comma
E	•	R	• — •	5	• • • • •	.	• — • — • —	period
F	• • — •	S	• • •	6	— • • • •	?	• • — — • •	question mark
G	— — •	T	—	7	— — • • •	;	— • — • —	semicolon
H	• • • •	U	• • —	8	— — — • •	:	— — — • • •	colon
I	• •	V	• • • —	9	— — — — •	/	— • • — •	slash
J	• — — —	W	• — —	0	— — — — —	-	— • • • • —	dash
K	— • —	X	— • • —	Á	• — — • —	'	• — — — — •	apostrophe
L	• — • •	Y	— • — —	Ä	• — • —	()	— • — — • —	parenthesis
M	— —	Z	— — • •	É	• • — • •	_	• • — — • —	underline

Á — A with accent · Ä — A with umlaut · É — E with accent

The River

Into each life a few tears must be shed.

For in order to keep the river of life flowing,

It must first be fed.

The river of life has many tributaries:

Some are great,

And some are small.

We are all bound to the river,

For the river of life flows through us all.

Sometimes the water can appear muddy

Due to storms,

Confusion,

And pain.

Other times the water is crystal clear,

Serene,

And very tame.

Your path along the river can be rocky at times.

Your path can be impassable at times,

Forcing you to detour,

Sometimes years out of the way.

Or your path may be plain and straight,

Cut from a bank of soft sand and smooth clay.

There are many things carried along by the river of life.

Flotsam, treasure, and trash. Dreams for the future, and shattered memories of the past. There are many bridges that span over the river of life.

Some are of iron, some are of wood, and others are of stone.

But the only bridges that truly matter are those of flesh and bone.

Chapter One

There Was a Time

There was a time when my world was fresh and new.

Life was simple;

When I could play all day without any rules.

There was a time when I didn't know how to read,

When all the words and sentences made no sense to me.

There was a time when I was in love.

I think about that time now and again.

I smile thinking how young and foolish I was back then.

There was a time when I was strong, when I felt invincible

When I was full of morals and principles.

There was a time when I wanted to help people;

I wanted to save lives as a team, or on my own.

But I couldn't save myself,

So the only life lost was that of my own.

There was a time.

Yes, there was a time.

I am writing this book while sitting in a wheelchair in front of a computer. Some readers may think, "Big deal! So he's disabled and he writes." I would agree if it weren't for the fact that I am not using my hands, nor am I using any kind of voice dictation software to write this book. One other fact that the readers of this book should know is that I am also blind. I am using Morse code that I tap out on a switch with my tongue.

I am writing this book for three reasons. First, I need something to occupy my time and writing gives me that outlet. Second, I want to help people. Perhaps my experiences could help others who may be in similar situations. Third, I want people to understand.

Chapter Two

The Reaper

Time is the best teacher,

For it kills all its students.

From the moment we are born, we begin to die.

Ashes to ashes.

Dust to dust.

If we choose to live, than die we must.

As we grow older

Our bodies become weaker.

Doctors may try to prolong your life,

But no one can outrun the reaper.

It was a cold, January morning in northern Minnesota. I woke up gasping for breath. It was about 5:00 AM. The feeble winter sun would not rise for a couple more hours. No matter, by the time the first rays crept over the eastern horizon, I would be dead. Sitting up, I turned on my bedside lamp and fumbled for my asthma inhaler. I brought it to my lips and took two quick puffs. I waited a minute and then took two more, trying desperately to force the medicine into my tight, wheezing lungs. After a minute, I got up to prepare a breathing treatment.

I was having a severe asthma attack. The short walk to my desk chair was taxing for me, but I stayed calm. I knew the drill. I had been through it all before, more times than I cared to remember. I had learned long ago not to panic, get scared, or start crying during an asthma attack. It just makes it ten times worse. It is hard to control your instinct to panic. It is a frightening sensation to not be able to breathe.

I sat down in my desk chair. It was actually a kitchen chair that I had hauled up to my room. The thing was an ugly pink with metal legs. I didn't care. It had a thick vinyl cushion. It may have looked like hell, but it was comfy. I began to prepare my breathing treatment, not knowing that this would be my last asthma attack. The year was 1992. I was seventeen years old, a senior in high school.

As I began to mix my saline and atropine cocktail, I remember thinking about all those poor bastards over in Iraq. There was a war going on, Operation Desert Storm. I remember hearing on the news about the threat of a chemical attack on the troops. The antidote for such an attack was atropine. There were not enough doses for all the soldiers, so the generals decided not to supply them with any. Anyway, that's what the TV said, so I felt a little guilty that I had this medicine. It came in a little glass vial that you had to extract with a syringe. The label said, "POISON: DO NOT DRINK." I wasn't going to drink it. Instead I poured it into my nebulizer machine. Then, placing a mask over my face, I turned the machine on and began trying to breathe in the mist.

Chapter Three

Asthma

No longer do I fear death;

I no longer struggle to take a breath.

No longer do I fear the dark night:

No longer do I need an inhaler to make it through the night.

No more pills, no more shots, and no more treatments to help me breathe;

I threw all my medicines away and now I am free.

Asthma is a disease that affects the lungs. It constricts the airways, or bronchial tubes, in the lungs. Most people outgrow it from childhood, but some aren't that lucky. An asthma attack feels like you are slowly suffocating. For example, try breathing through a drinking straw. Now slowly bend the straw in half. It is now harder to breathe. You have to fight for each breath. That is sort of what an asthma attack feels like. Sometimes, I would have as many as three attacks a day. There are a lot of different things that can trigger an asthma attack: allergies, exertion, humidity, or even catching a cold. All of these things affected me to a certain extent.

Chapter Four

Hitchhiking to the Afterlife

Hitchhiking to the afterlife.

You can take my thumbs, and you can take my hands.

Go on and take them; I'll understand.

You can take my toes; you can take my feet.

I won't mind, not in the least.

You might as well take my eyes and my ears.

They won't do me much good, sitting around here.

You can yank out my tongue; you can pull out my teeth.

There's no more to say, no reason to speak.

There's nothing left for you to take.

Now, across the river Styx I will make.

You can take it all; you can take my life.

I'm hitchhiking to the afterlife.

My medicine wasn't helping. The breathing treatment didn't help, neither did my inhaler that was almost empty. I was in trouble. Just then, there was a knock at my bedroom door. It was my dad. He had seen my light when he went out to put wood in the furnace. The winters in northern Minnesota were long, cold affairs. Many people burned wood to heat their homes. He came in to see if I was all right.

I told him that I needed the doctor. By this time it was difficult for me to even speak. The word hospital would have required too much air to say, air that I didn't have, but I managed to squeak out the word *doctor* somehow. My dad left to go warm up the car. Then, getting shakily to my feet, I pulled on a pair of jeans and headed down the stairs. I remember having to brace myself against the wall as I descended. My knees were wobbly. I felt like a hundred-year-old drunk person.

I made it down the stairs and into the kitchen, holding on to the countertop to keep from falling. I remember trying to concentrate on what was in front of me. My brother's wallet and car keys, an old coffee cup full of pens and pencils, and an old phone with the cord all stretched out. I still gripped my inhaler tightly in my hand. It had become sort of a security blanket for me. I never went anywhere without it, for it had saved me so many times before. But now it didn't seem to be helping.

My mom was the only one in the kitchen. Everyone else was still asleep. My dad came in to say that the car was ready. Shuffling slowly forward, weaving unsteadily like a drunken old man, I made my way to the front door where I slipped into my tennis shoes and then tried to shrug into my leather bomber jacket. My mom and dad had to help. I liked that jacket. I was proud of the fact that I bought it with my own money, so it pissed me off when the paramedics had to cut it to pieces.

As I stepped outside, I immediately lapsed into a coughing fit as the cold air bit into my lungs. Even though my dad had the foresight to pull the car a few yards from the front door, I still had difficulty climbing inside. The nearest hospital was about fifteen miles away. It usually took about ten minutes doing eighty miles per hour the whole way, but, on the icy snow-covered highway, it was going to take a bit longer. A bit too long, as it turned out. I wasn't going to make it in time.

As we sped down the dark, cold highway, the snow and ice crunching beneath the tires, the headlights shone over the ghostly white snow banks and the rows of naked dark trees. I brought my inhaler to my lips one last time and pushed the button repeatedly, but it was no use; it was empty. My dad laid his hand on my shoulder. I think he was trying to tell me to hang on. I was in no shape to reply. The car remained silent. I thought, just a little further and I would be okay. We were about halfway to the hospital. I remember passing the lighted billboard of the hardware store. Then I took my last breath, slipping away into the darkness

Chapter Five

Many things

I have been many different things during my life. I was a son and a brother; I was a hunter and a fisherman. I worked as a field hand; I was a roofer and a cook. I was an artist and a poet; I was an inventor. I was a rock climber; I was a VCR and a TV antenna repair person. I was a kayaker. I was a first-responder. I was also a vegetable. I was all these things and only seventeen years old.

My name is Joshua LaRue. I was born in northern Minnesota in 1974. I grew up in an old house on the south shore of a small lake. Now, when I say old house, I mean the thing was pretty old. In fact, it was over 130 years old, and it was built solid and is still standing to this day. Within that old house was a hundred years of accumulated dust, mold, old paint, old insulation, and God knows what else. I think that is one of the reasons I had so many respiratory problems growing up.

Growing up, I was sick a lot of the time. When I was seven years old, the doctors diagnosed me with asthma. I was in and out of the hospital more times than I care to remember. The first time I was admitted to the hospital, I was scared to death. I did not want to be there; I wanted to go home. I wanted my mom. I lay there crying under the stiff white sheets. A nurse asked me if I wanted some dinner. They were serving tacos, but I was too scared to eat. I remember that first trip to the hospital plain as day. Needless to say, I missed a lot of school. It seemed like I was always playing catch-up. I was a fast learner, and for the most part I did my best to keep up.

For me, asthma was a nuisance. My dad was always telling me to take it easy. Boy, I hated that. One time, my elementary teacher called my parents' house. She was concerned because I had missed something like five Mondays, in a row, of school. She wanted to know if something was going on. It wasn't that I didn't want to go to school. It was just that after playing hard all weekend, I would often be too sick to go due to the frequent asthma attacks. It seemed like the older I got, the fewer asthma attacks I had, but at the same time, they seemed to be growing in severity. In spite of all that, I was a very active kid. I enjoyed hunting, fishing, water-skiing, swimming, snowshoeing, kayaking, mountain biking, and rock climbing. I also enjoyed wood-carving. I was starting to get pretty good until I took my last breath.. Now, all my knives are put away. The few carvings I have left sit in a box on a shelf in my closet. I had given most of the good ones away as presents.

Chapter Six

Rocks

I have been stranded upon an angry sea.

My lifeboat is lost.

I am so far from the shore.

Oh please, won't someone come and rescue me?

Throw me a lifeline.

Hold my hand.

Pull me up out of this darkness and choking brine.

I want to stand in the warm sunlight, one last time.

My life was once whole.

My future was so bright.

My plans were set.

But the winds of fate blew my ship of dreams, way off-course.

I sailed into blackness, into a fog.

I didn't know which way to go.

I was confused and lost,

sailing blindly forward

until my hopes and dreams were smashed to pieces upon the rocks.

Since I was in and out of the hospital so much as a kid, I got to know the emergency room personnel pretty well. The respiratory techs and paramedics were all nice people. Sometimes they would stop by my hospital room to visit. We would talk about fishing or basketball or they would show me some card tricks, like how to cut a deck of cards with one hand. It really meant a lot to me that they took the time to do that. I looked up to them; their job was to save lives. I wanted to be like them, not knowing that in a few years they would be the ones saving my life.

When I was seventeen, my friend Ryan and I enrolled in a First Responder course at the hospital. First Responder was a class in advanced first aid, which trained members of various volunteer fire departments and other volunteers what to do when arriving at the scene of an accident, especially how to stabilize the patient until an ambulance arrived. That was the role of a first responder. It was a forty-hour course that we attended two evenings each week. The class covered many areas of first aid from treating cuts and broken bones: to how to treat a sucking chest wound, or even how to deliver a baby in an emergency. The class was held in the dining room of the nursing home that was connected to the hospital. There would often be the lingering odor of stewed prunes and pureed meat loaf in the air as we took our seats; at least, that's what I thought it smelled like.

I had a plan. I wanted to be a paramedic. This class would be my first step. I would take more classes and become an EMT. Then I would go to college and take even more classes, and eventually become a paramedic. That was my plan. However, my life did not turn out as I had planned. In fact, after passing my final test for the class, I would find myself back at the same hospital, less than twelve hours later. I returned, not as a student, but as a patient fighting for my life. I eventually became a resident of the hospital's nursing home, the same nursing home where I used to volunteer.

Chapter Seven

My Soul

Falling through the keyhole of life, I lost my direction in space
and time, losing consciousness as the nightmares and visions plague
my mind. I try to walk, but I stumble and fall. I can see myself lying
motionless and not moving at all.

Heaven won't take me and hell don't want me. Not without a soul.
Have you seen it? It's about six feet tall and as black as coal.

It slipped away when I was not aware, and the doctor tossed it away
without a care. I've searched every room in the house and behind every
door. Have you seen it? It's about six foot tall and black to the core.

I lost my soul somewhere along the way, when the doctor threw it
away. I've been searching up and down, left and right. Have you seen
it? It's six foot tall and black as night.

My soul, my soul. Has anyone seen my soul?

There are many details of my last day that still stick out in my mind. I remember going to school and getting a detention slip for skipping school, to go ice fishing with my buddy Joe. I had two dollars and sixty-eight cents in my pants pocket. When my mom collected my clothes from the emergency room, she found that blue slip of paper, along with a Rolling Stones tape, in my jacket pocket.

I remember going to visit my boss at the electronic repair shop after Ryan and I passed the First Responder test. I remember riding in the car with Ryan and telling him that I wished we had some alcohol to celebrate.

I remember standing in my boss's living room as he told us *good job*. I remember going home and telling my parents I was a first responder now and my mom telling me she was proud of me. I remember going down to the basement to work on my kayak that was lying across the ping-pong table. I had been in the process of refurbishing it: sanding it down and fiber-glassing some spots.

I remember waking up unable to breathe. I remember every detail of that morning, until I passed the lights of the hardware store. Then I was gone. Afterwards I would replay that morning over in my mind a thousand times, trying to think of something that I could have done different, some little detail that I had overlooked that could have saved me. For a long time I felt like a failure. Just the night before I had been trained to help people and to save lives. Now here I was, stuck in a car racing to the hospital, helpless to even save myself. By that time, I had stopped breathing. I was not aware of the white froth issuing from my nose and mouth. Nor was I aware of the car speeding into the parking lot of the Super America gas station, or of being dragged from the car as a complete stranger named Bruce gave me CPR until the ambulance arrived. I was not aware of the paramedics as they cut off the arm of my jacket to search for a vein for the IV needle.

I did not register any of those things because I was clinically dead. The next thing I knew, I found myself standing in a long passageway or corridor. I don't know how I got there. One minute I was sitting in the front seat of the car, and then suddenly the next thing I knew I was someplace else. The passageway, or whatever it was, was dimly lit. The walls and floor seemed to be made of stone. I remember starting to walk forward, down the silent, dim corridor. The only noise that could be heard was the sound of my breathing and the echoing footfalls of my shoes. I still could not breathe; I felt like I was suffocating. In truth, that is what was happening. With each step, I could feel myself becoming weaker. After I had walked some distance, I noticed a figure standing up ahead. I remember trying to call out to it, pleading with it to help me. I was begging it to help me. I was saying, "help me, I am dying," over and over. But it never responded to me. As I drew closer, I saw that the figure was tall. I could not tell if it was a man or a woman. Its face was hidden. It seemed to be wearing the outfit of a pilot, possibly from

World War I. It wore tall leather boots, black ones, and brown and tan old-fashioned trousers.

It wore what looked to be a large leather jacket. Its hands were encased in leather gloves. It had a long scarf wound about its neck. I think it was either gray or white. Its eyes were covered by big goofy-looking goggles, and atop its head was a leather helmet. I don't know if the figure was a pilot or if it was just death waiting for me in disguise. Never once did it try to speak to me. It just stood there coldly, watching me in silence. Stumbling forward, I was about ten yards from the figure when I collapsed on the cold stone floor. I tried to get up, but I was too weak to even raise my head. I lay motionless, sprawled face-first on the cold, hard floor.

After awhile, I was aware of the sensation of being picked up and carried by three other figures. They brought me to a long white table or bed. They stood over me, but I could not see their faces. I pleaded with them,, "Please help me—I'm dying". They spoke to me, but I could not understand their words. I was in agony. I never felt so awful in my entire life. Then everything seemed to stop, as if time were standing still. I then felt something touch my chest ever so softly, like a puff of air or a cotton ball dropped on my chest. The feeling was so imperceptible that it is hard to put into words. I didn't know what was happening. I opened my eyes and suddenly everything had changed. I sat up in bed, then swinging my legs over the side, I stood up. The first thing that I noticed was the total lack of pain. I didn't realize just how much pain I was in until that moment. So it felt strange not feeling any at all. I felt so good. I was in good shape before from hours of paddling a boat, mountain biking, and rock climbing. I was pretty strong, but now I felt as if I had the strength of ten men.

I was five foot eleven at the time, and weighed between 155 and 160 pounds. My hair was light brown and curly; my eyes were dark brown with some flecks of green.

As I stood there, I was looking all around. It's hard to explain, but somehow it just all felt natural to me. Glancing over, I could see my body lying on the bed. That was pretty strange, let me tell you! I knew what I was seeing, but somehow it didn't matter. I felt like the body lying on the bed was just an empty shell. Like a deflated balloon or an empty package. It was as if my body were something to discard, as though it were no longer needed. I was aware of a light around me. It wasn't a bright light; it was more like the soft buttery glow of candlelight. In this light there was such a profound feeling of peace and love that there are no words to describe it. It was the most beautiful light that I had ever seen. Raising my hands to my face, I discovered the light was coming from me. I could see through my hands as if they were made from the light. My whole body was made of the light. I felt warm and safe, wrapped up in peaceful love. I can't describe how I felt. There are no words. I was happy. I was laughing to myself, for I had just got the joke. People go through their entire lives fearing death, fighting to prolong their lives as long as possible. I know I fought like hell to stay alive. People fear the unknown. I know there are people who think that I am nuts when I say death is nothing to be afraid of. Why fear something that is going to happen to all of us eventually? You can't stop or prevent it from happening. It's a part of life. The process of dying can be truly horrible and awful, but death is nothing to be afraid of. I somehow knew I was dead. I can't explain it, but it all seemed to be okay. I wasn't scared or angry. I felt happy and relieved, as if a great weight had been lifted from my shoulders.

As I turned away from my body, I saw that there was a staircase before me. The stairs were wide and smooth, leading upwards. I began climbing them. I was thinking of my family as I climbed the stairs. I knew that they would all miss me, but something told me—it was a very strong feeling that I had—that they would be all right. I continued climbing. When I had climbed a dozen steps, I turned back to look at my body. It was still there, right where I had left it lying on the bed. I turned around again to continue climbing. That is when everything crashed back, and I was swallowed up by a tidal wave of confusion and pain.

Chapter Eight

Mirrors

I am lost in a wilderness of mirrors.

I can't tell which is truth and which are lies.

All of the reflections look the same to my blind eyes.

I can't tell which way is up, which way is down.

I no longer can tell if I am moving to my left or right.

I am lost in a confused mass of shadow and light.

The facets of my life have been shattered beyond repair.

My broken dreams cut so painfully deep.

To bleed away hope, only to be replaced by my haunted sleep.

I am lost here in this wilderness of mirrors.

There is no escape.

There is no way out, imprisoned in my own frozen reflection here I

remain stuck.

Surrounded on all sides, by so much potential bad luck. I was alive. I didn't know where I was or what had happened. There was all this pain and noise all around me, so much pain. People were shouting so loud; it was hurting my ears. I wanted to tell them to stop it and be quiet. When I tried to open my mouth to speak, no words would come out. I found that I could not talk. I felt myself moving. I was being wheeled on some kind of bed very rapidly. Then a face loomed above me. I saw it was a woman. She was wearing a short-sleeved shirt with patches sewn on the front. I assumed that she was either an EMT or a paramedic, but I didn't know at the time. She was leaning over me and she was shouting at me. I was pretty out of it by then. She was telling me that I had an asthma attack. I thought to myself, "what asthma attack?" What was she talking about, was she crazy? I didn't remember any asthma attack. I stared blankly up at her wondering to myself if she knew that I could see down the front of her shirt. I had not lost my eyesight yet; that would come later.

I was confused and tired, so very tired. They say that the brain starts to die or fry after six minutes without oxygen. I don't know how true that is. For I have heard of skin divers that were able to hold their breath for seven minutes. Nevertheless, it turned out that I had gone without oxygen for far too long. The doctors estimated somewhere in the ballpark of ten to fifteen minutes. I felt hands under me, lifting me up. Then it all came back to me in a rush: I remembered everything that had happened. The realization hit me all at once. I didn't have time to process any of it before I slipped into unconsciousness. I then fell into a coma, where I would linger for nearly three months. I did not know what fresh hell awaited me, alone in the darkness.

A coma is like a black fog in your brain. It is like a nightmare you cannot wake from. Imagine being stuck in a deep, dark well, where you could not crawl out of or even cry out for help. That is the position I found myself in for nearly three months: unable to move, half-dead, and half-asleep. I lay in my hospital bed, on life support and in critical condition. They cut a hole in my neck to place a breathing tube called a tracheostomy tube (often referred to as a trake tube), and hooked me up to all kinds of tubes and machines. I was transferred to a hospital in the Twin Cities, and I was hooked up to their life support equipment. The doctors didn't think I was going to make it. My parents, aunts, uncles, brothers, and cousins all gathered around my hospital room. They weren't sure if I was going to make it either. I guess they wanted to see me and also wanted a chance to say good-bye, if it came to that. I was a sick puppy. One of my brothers told me later that when everyone gathered around my hospital bed, I apparently coughed so hard that I hit my uncle in the chest with a big glob of phlegm from across the room. I (of course) thought that must have seemed pretty funny. I don't remember much of that time for I was somewhere else.

It might sound crazy but I left my body behind many times during those first few weeks. I remember sitting in the hospital waiting room with my brothers on the morning of my accident. I was really laying in the emergency room, but somehow I found myself sitting among my brothers in the waiting room. I remember hearing what sounded like the noise of an airplane propeller starting up outside the glass doors. I remember wanting to take a ride on that plane. I had an urgent feeling that I had to leave. I remember getting up from my chair, where I sat looking at magazines. There was a *Newsweek* that had a pretty cool picture of an egg cracking on the front cover. Getting up from my chair, I walked to the glass doors. I couldn't see outside; it was pitch black. There were no streetlights burning or even headlights from any passing cars.

As I stood at those doors, the noise seemed to be getting louder and louder, as if the airplane was taxiing outside the doors. But I was not able to see any plane in the dark. As I turned away to return to my seat, the noise died down. Later, I found out that I had been air-lifted by helicopter. I remember asking my older brother to tell our mom that I had to leave. I told him to call her to see if I could take a plane ride. I really wanted to get on that plane. I had a strange feeling like I was invited to go and somehow I was expected to go along, but he didn't seem to hear me.

Sitting there in the waiting room, I watched as the fluorescent lights overhead cast a dull gleam on the checkerboard tile that disappeared around the corner of the hallway. Along one wall, there were framed portraits hanging. The pictures were of some of the staff: the doctors and paramedics. Doubtless, they were some of the same people who were, at that moment, trying to save my life. Further down, at the end of the hall, were two payphones mounted on the wall. I found myself standing in front of the phones. I wanted so badly to leave. But somehow it was important that I say good-bye to my mom first. I stood there in front of the phones, wanting to call my mom and dad, when everything went black once again.

The next time I remember leaving my body behind was when I woke up back in my own room. I was back in my old house, in my old bedroom. I remember getting out of bed and turning on both lights. It was so dark; the shadows seemed to cling to everything. I remember walking across the short hallway to my brother's room. His room was black. I turned the light on. All his things were there, but he wasn't in bed. I crossed the hall to my sister's room and pushed the door open. I saw that her room was also black. Turning on her light, I saw that she also was not there. Returning to the hall, I turned on the light at the top of the stairs and then headed down the steps. Upon reaching the bottom, I walked over to turn on the switch for the living room light. After I turned that on, I crossed the floor to my parents' room.

After knocking, I pushed the door open. Their room was also black and empty. I wandered through the whole house, turning on every light switch I could find: the bathroom, the kitchen, and the pantry. I eventually turned on every light in the entire house. I was so hot and thirsty. I felt like I was burning up. I felt like I had been out in the hot desert sun for days with no water.

I wanted desperately to find something to quench my thirst. Pulling open the refrigerator door, I stood there letting the cold air wash over me. Gazing up, I spotted a gallon-sized milk jug full of sun tea. Hooking my fingers through the handle, I dragged the container out of the fridge. I tried wrestling it to the counter, but for some reason the jug seemed very heavy. I went for a glass, reaching in the cupboard. Fumbling around, I finally managed to seize a glass between my palms, which I carefully set down on the counter. My hands did not want to work. I tried to pick up the jug to pour tea into the glass, but it was too heavy. I couldn't lift it. I was so thirsty but being unable to pour a simple glass of tea was beyond frustration. I thought what I needed was some sort of straw that I could stick down in the jug. I knew we didn't have any straws in the house, but I thought maybe I could improvise. I walked over to the cup that held the pens and pencils. My idea was to try to take apart a pen to make a straw. All that the cup held were pencils and one pen, but it was the clicky kind, and I couldn't get it apart with my teeth. I needed a new plan. Crossing to the kitchen sink I turned on the spigot. I tried cupping my hands to get a drink, but my hands no longer seemed to work. I tried sticking my head under it, but it was too big and wouldn't fit. Feeling frustrated and so parched by thirst, I headed outside to try the outside faucet. Stepping outside was like walking into a black fog. There were no stars and no moon. There was no longer a security light in the front yard. It may have been there, but it was way too dark to see. It was like being in a cave. I could not see my hand in front of my face. The only light that could be seen came from two tall torches that sat on either side of the driveway. I walked over to take a closer look. The two torches cast small pools of light onto the gravel drive. That's all there was; there was no snow. Everything else—the grass and trees—were all lost in the darkness. For some reason, I didn't want to walk any further than the torches, so I turned back to the house. But when I turned around, the house wasn't there. It looked as if it were being consumed behind a wall of flames. Then everything went black, once again.

Chapter Nine

Mind's Eye

I see the world in a very different way than most people.

My eyes are broken; my eyes are blind.

But somehow I can still see through my mind's eye.

Sometimes I see things that no one else sees.

Sometimes I see things that I don't understand—

A fleeting glimpse of the future out of the corner of my

      eye.

I use to think I was crazy, I thought I was losing my mind.

I didn't realize that I was looking through my mind's eye.

I have seen things that people won't believe.

Most of them would laugh and scoff.

I told them I have seen angels, and I have seen devils and

      the face of God.

I try to see the beauty in all things.

Some beautiful people are ugly,

Some ugly people are beautiful,

It all depends on how they act and what they say.

There were several more instances where I seemed to leave my body behind, but I do not wish to mention them here for two reasons: first, people would find it unbelievable, and second, they were not all pleasant. I will just tell you that I saw things that I could not explain. I saw places that I had never seen before, places that I would eventually end up at later in life. Be it by chance or accident.

Chapter Ten

Silent Tears

Pinned to the earth, the landslide washes over me. My thoughts turn inward. My thoughts turn black. I am swallowed up. I am buried alive as a mountain of grief crashes down upon me. The dam to my heart has burst. The floodgate to my emotions has been washed aside. As twin rivers of tears flow from my eyes, to escape into madness, to leave reality behind. O life can be cruel. Life can be so unkind at times when grief is so fresh and raw. Mingled with sadness and pain. It's enough to put someone over the edge and drive the sanest of people insane. Trapped somewhere between heaven and hell. Caught between two worlds. In the light of day and in the dark of night my soul yearns to escape. To journey on its endless flight. But here I remain. Pinned to the earth with no end in sight. People say that I am lucky to be alive, but nobody notices, as the silent tears fall from my eyes.

After awhile, the doctors determined that I was going to make it. I was disconnected from the life support equipment, and allowed to breathe on my own, though I still had a tracheostomy tube stuck in my neck. I was also connected to a feeding tube. They disconnected me from one tube only to be hooked up to something else it seemed. The feeding tube consisted of a short rubber tube that was inserted into my stomach, about two inches above my belly button. They would take a large syringe and fill it with this vile- smelling crap. I think it was something like *Ensure*. All I can tell you is that it tasted awful. I never drank it, but I could taste it whenever I burped. They would fit this syringe onto the hose, slowly empting the contents into my stomach. For the next few months, I would be fed this way most of the time. It was a weird sensation, especially if the stuff was cold. Still in a deep coma, I was transferred back up north to the same nursing home where I had taken my First Responders classes. I was no longer a student; instead, I was to become one of the residents of the care center.

I don't remember much of the first few weeks I spent in the nursing home. Maybe it's a good thing that I don't, for I imagine that I was in pretty bad shape. I know that when I first got there that I shared a room with someone else. I don't recall the man's name; it might have been something like Howard or Howie. In any case, what I do remember about him was that he used to yell—constantly. I am not sure what was the matter with him. It could have been dementia; I don't know.

What I do remember was that he would scream at the top of his lungs like a giant baby throwing a temper tantrum. When he would bellow, it sounded like some kind of baby elephant. I used to have nightmares about being chased by half-man, half-elephant creatures. Then I would wake up and find him screaming.

I was unconscious: I could not move, I could not speak, nor could I see. I had just suffered a severe TBI or Traumatic Brain Injury. I was seventeen years old, and I was stuck in a nursing home. I was helpless. But somehow I managed to cling to life. Scrambling by tooth and nail, I fought back, desperate to hang on to my life. Maybe if I had known what awaited me? If I would have just known how much frustration and pain lay ahead I would have given up and slipped silently and painlessly away into the darkness. But how was I to know? Hindsight is truly 20/20. I was a prisoner in my own mind; my coma was my prison cell. In the weeks and months ahead, I would slowly emerge from my dark prison only to be confronted by a new nightmare of finding myself mute, paralyzed, and blind. My mom had the foresight to leave a notebook for visitors to write in by my bedside. This notebook chronicles the start of my slow and painful recovery.

Chapter Eleven

Seventeen Inside

The raven croaks and the loon cries.

The sun turned black and the stars all died.

The day I left your side.

I was only seventeen inside.

My family gathered around my bedside.

As the doctors told how my brain was fried.

My mother wept, and my fathered cried.

I was only seventeen inside.

I was in a bad place.

I was so hot and thirsty.

My cracked lips bled, for my mouth was so dry.

I could not move, because my hands were tied.

I was only seventeen inside.

I would wake up from the pain.

I would scream in agony.

It would all be in vain.

For no one heard me, no one came.

Then I would pass out from the pain once again.

People came and people went.

Sometimes they would sit and talk to me for a time.

I was only seventeen inside.

I was a senior in high school.

I should have been going to parties, having the time of my life.

But while my friends were going to the prom,

I was fighting for my life.

I was only seventeen inside.

I cheated death a second time; I beat the odds.

I am still alive.

But I don't feel much like celebrating.

I have been to hell.

Know I have to live with the effects, for the rest of my life.

I was only seventeen inside.

February 20, 1992

I don't remember very much of my early stay at the nursing home; I was still pretty out of it. I was still in a coma, plus I was on a lot of medication at that time. I found out later that it was something like eleven different medications. I have no idea what the drugs were, or what, if any, long-term side effects they may have caused me. If they led to my loss of vision, I don't know. All I know is that I was only seventeen, and I was in no position to question anyone's judgment.

The only bright spot of my stay was that I got a lot of visitors: family, friends from school, neighbors, and also people I worked with. Even some people I had never met before came to see me. These are some of their entries:

February 20, 1992

Snowed today, mom was here, blinked twice, and looked at poster and mom and plants. Sat up in chair 7:15 PM, 'Josh looked at me for awhile—not a long time, but awhile. Yesterday he did a lot. Around 9:00 PM Sara came.

Sara was a friend from school. She also worked at the place next door to where I worked. She worked at the Garrison Animal Hospital as a veterinary assistant. At that time I worked for the vet's husband at the electronic repair shop next-door.

February 21, 1992

"Mom not feeling well, dad here today. P.T. Nurse encouraged by response when working with Josh. He didn't like it. Josh had his first bath today about 10:30, went well. He looks refreshed".

February 22, 1992

9:00 PM

Jack Vooge:

"Josh is more alert than I have ever seen him. Opening his eyes wide, will blink fast when I ask him to. He will squeeze my hand when I ask him to. When I asked him if he wanted some water he would open his mouth. Nurses came in and put on his "gear," then he started to fight a lot and arch his back. Nurses untied his arms and he calmed down and went to sleep."

I was still in a coma at this time. I could hear people talking, but it was like being half asleep all the time. For some reason, the nurses would tie my hands to the bed. I remember waking with my hands tied in these big mittens and not being able to move. I didn't know where I was or what was happening. I remember one time waking up face down in my hospital bed pillow, I struggled to move but I was so weak. I finally managed to move my head so I could breathe. The air never smelled so sweet. I know that if I had died, the nurses would have lied and said that I had died in my sleep.

February 23, 1992

Sunday

"Thirsty, hot, sleepy and frustrated, Mom."

February 23, 1992

4:00 PM

"Dad with Josh resting okay. I love you so much I can't stand to see you this way." My Dad had a hard time seeing me in pain. I imagine he felt helpless. I don't think any parent wants to watch their child suffer.

February 23, 1992.

5:45 PM.

"Me (Shannon) and Carrie stopped by. You opened your eyes quite a bit: we woke you up. You had a couple of those lemon sticks. We could see the emotion in your face Josh, WAKE UP SOON JOSH! WE LOVE AND MISS YOU! We gave you that little sponge with water in it. You loved it; you tried to bite off a piece of skin on your lip. I am sure you will get it off sooner or later."

The nurses would not give me anything to drink. I think they were afraid I would choke. I was so unbelievably thirsty. All they would give me were these lemon mouth swabs that tasted like furniture polish. As they swabbed my mouth and my cracked, bleeding lips, I would try to bite the sponge in an attempt to suck a few more drops of moisture into my parched mouth. I know it was a reflex action on my part. The nurses would get mad and take it away. I remember opening my mouth and sticking out my tongue to show that I was thirsty. But the nurses didn't notice me. If it weren't for my visitors, I'm not sure that I would ever have gotten anything to drink.

February 23, 1992
5:45 PM

"You listened to We Can Work It Out *first done by the Beatles, but you heard the version by Tesla. You listened to a tape by Poison. You and Joe always used to sing* Unskinny Bop *last summer. Whenever I was with you guys, you were listening to that tape. You listened to other songs by Tesla. See Ya!* "Love Shannon, Love Carrie". Shannon and Carrie are friends from school.

February 23, 1992
8:00 PM

"Jack, Deb & Sara stopped by. "He is the most alert we have ever seen him (he hasn't had any Adavan since Friday). He looks at us when we talk to him. Gets aggravated & frustrated very easily."

I could not talk or tell anyone that I was in pain. When I would get agitated, the nurses would give me a shot of Adavan to knock me out.

February 24, 1992

"Snowed, Josh sleeping, as he was awake most of the night. Going to start recovery therapy next week. Put Josh in special chair, rolled him out to the sun room and mom cut his hair."

I had not had a shave or a haircut for awhile. I had a pretty good mustache growing by then.

February 24, 1992

6:00 PM

"I (Noelle) stopped to see you, you were wide awake. You were so alert, always wanting water. I put your glasses on and you watched me as I read to you. We listened to music and you looked so peaceful—not fretting around, the best I have seen you in days. Keep fighting Joshua, you are doing so good! Love Noelle

P.S. you shook your head no to me when I asked if you wanted your glasses off".

I had worn contacts and glasses at the time, though they no longer helped me to see. I think that it may have been comforting to have them on.

February 24, 1992

9:30 PM

(Jack V)

"Josh is very alert. He will respond and fight every time I call to him. He is fighting it so much that he is hot and sweaty. I wonder if that is good or bad."

I was in a lot of pain. I had constant muscle spasms and cramps in my legs. It felt like my legs were covered in charley horses. It felt as if every nerve in my body was raw and on fire. Everything I felt and heard, felt somehow magnified one thousand percent. Jack would sometimes talk very loud, assuming that I could not hear, when in fact, I now seemed to have super-human hearing. He didn't know that he was hurting my ears.

February 26, 1992

36ᵗʰ day

Weather is sunny going up to the 40's Josh sleeping this afternoon. Chest X-ray, infection. Dad and I here to see you. Dad going home to paint the hall. Gave Josh some Dr. Pepper that really made his eyes open.

I got pneumonia from lying in bed so much.

February 26, 1992

Wednesday

Stopped in to say hi before I left for Alaska. I really felt Josh recognized who I was. He seemed to shake my hand, tried hard to focus on me. Always in my prayers, Jason Bernier.

Jason was my neighbor. I did recognize him, but could not talk to let him know. He was a good guy.

February 26, 1992

9:15 PM

(Jack V)

Josh about the same. Opens his eyes when you call to him. Makes a face and fights for awhile. Sweating a lot and is very thirsty. Sara and I gave him lots of water and pop.

I had a fever from the pneumonia. I was so thirsty and could not get enough liquids.

February 27, 1992

(Mom) Josh is running a fever, very thirsty, looking all around. Getting meds to relax him.

February 27, 1992

3:00 PM to 4:45 PM

You were sleeping when we got here, very hot. You only opened your eyes a few times. I gave you a little bit of Dr. Pepper, but you were not very thirsty. We arm-wrestled and you beat me! Boy was I surprised. We miss you, Joshua. Love Noelle and Raelynn

P.S. Vindy and Nora came and left while we were here.

Noelle, Raelynn, Vindy and Nora were friends from school.

March 4, 1992

9:00 PM

(Jack V)

"Josh was very sweaty and crooked in bed like he was fighting a lot. I put a cool towel on his forehead and talked to him for awhile. He calmed down and rested for awhile. He seemed to have more control over his arms than before. I asked him to blink if he could hear me and he did. I asked him to squeeze my hand and he did. I gave him lots of water, he was very thirsty. He stayed calm for awhile and then when the guy in the other room started shouting, he opened his eyes and started moving and fighting a lot. He seemed to be trying to break through with all his might. His heart is beating very hard and fast and his temp seems high".

March 7, 1992

"Rain again (mom) Josh is very alert today looks right at you. Doctor tested him too. Sleeping now, out of ICU last night across the hall again. No fever, cool.

Tanya and Shannon stopped in to see you. You woke up right away and you were looking right at us. You got to get up and get your blonde hair and dark tan back. I know you can do it. We love you Tanya and Shannon p.s. he smiled."

March 8, 1992

"Dad, mom, brother Jed and uncle Carl were here. Sat you up in a chair for a half hour, turns to our voices really great. Please put tape on for Josh when you leave, thanks."

My mom's taste in music was very different from mine. She would play her religious tapes in my room. It wasn't my choice of music, but I was now her captive audience, so I had to suffer in silence.

March 9, 1992

"Cold and sunny. Dad, Grandma and Aunt Diane up to see Josh. Resting but wakes up, looks around, alert."

Not thirsty, my fever was about gone. I found out later that it had got up to 106 while I was in the ICU. I was very weak and tired.

"Matt, Leighton, Shannon and Joe came to see you. You were awake for awhile. Arm-wrestled with Leighton, you were pretty tired or you would have beat Leighton. Right!!"

Matt, Leighton, and Joe were friends from school.

Tuesday March 10, 1992

"Cold, sunny (mom) Josh moved back to his room in care center. All say how much better he looks. He is resting this afternoon, listening to the radio."

I remember they were giving away a trip for two if you answered the right question on the radio. If I had been able to talk on the phone, I might have won. When I fell asleep, I dreamt of tropical beaches.

March 19, 1992

"The Marx family here. We finally realized this book is here! Just a little slow. Josh is resting peacefully. He opened his eyes when we talked to him but he seems sleepy. Love you Josh."

I used to work for the Marks'; they hired most of the kids in the neighborhood to work in their strawberry fields. They were good people.

March 23, 1992

9:30 PM

(Jack V),

"Josh shocked me tonight, when I came in the room I just started talking right away about how I stopped and talked to his mom today, and how Rusty came up and started sniffing my leg like he was going to pee on me again. Right away he started smiling and laughing! We also had a conversation: we decided that no is headshake for no (back and forth) and yes is eyes shut for a few seconds. He started making faces and struggling, and I asked him if he had pain, he gave me the yes signal. I asked him if it was his stomach, he gave me the no signal. I asked if it was his legs and he gave me the yes signal. I then looked at them, and they were in a very uncomfortable-looking position. I straightened them out and asked him if that was better, and he said yes. He seemed much more calm. After awhile, he went into his struggling again and he said he has severe pain in his legs."

It felt so good to finally have a conversation, even limited as it was with just yes and no answers. Nevertheless, we made it work. I laughed for the first time in a long time that night, picturing my dog, an English springer spaniel named Rusty, trying to pee on my boss's leg. When I laughed, I awoke from my coma for the first time. In the days that followed I seemed to awaken a little more each day, as the black fog slowly receded from my brain. I was still very weak and tired easily, but now I would be awake for longer periods of time.

March 24, 1992

7:40 AM

"Cheryl with respiratory: Walked in to do Josh's trake care this morning to find him ready to eat his first solid foods long awaited, did just great. He liked the Jell-O and the cranberry juice and 7Up. Did not care for the orange juice or the applesauce. I had to make this entry for you, I'm glad I was here to see it. Great! Good! And another big step! Cheryl"

I was finally allowed to eat some soft foods, like mashed potatoes and Jell-O. I had to learn how to do many things all over again; eating was no exception. The food at the nursing home was not very appealing; it was like eating baby food.

March 24, 1992

" Josh went outside today."

I got to sit outside in the fresh air, away from the unpleasant smells of the nursing home. It was the first time I had been able to sit outside since my accident. It was a March spring day in Minnesota. I sat there in my wheelchair taking everything in. I could not see my surroundings, but my other senses seemed to have become super acute to where I could form a picture of things in my mind's eye. For instance, there were still a few ragged piles of snow dotting the blacktop parking lot. There was a large diesel truck idling off to my right, in front of the glass doors of the waiting room. There I could hear the rumble of the motor and smell its exhaust as it drifted on the wind. I never thought truck exhaust could smell good, but things smell different after you have been cooped up in a nursing home for a couple of months. There was a road in front of me; I could hear the cars passing by as their tires splashed through the slushy water.

Beyond the road, there was a line of tall trees. Perched atop the top most branches sat a flock of about a dozen crows. They were squawking and cawing, making an excited and noisy racket. Even though I could not see the things around me, my remaining senses let me know where they were. The sun was warm on my upturned face. I sat there with the breeze blowing through my hair. The air was cool, carrying with it the smell of wet things. The spring air smelled like moldy wet hay, as the snow receded from the woods and fields, and from the brown dead grass of people's lawns.

March 27, 1992, a.m.

"Josh upset—distressed during respiratory treatment—finally slept. Getting cable hook up for a TV for him. Splint being ordered for left hand. The TV seems to upset him. Ryan A. came for a visit this afternoon."

The TV gave me nightmares. I remember watching the shows Mash and Star Trek. I don't know what drugs I was on, but it was like I was inside the TV. It's hard to explain, but it was like I was trapped inside the picture. It was very scary. I still could not talk, to tell them to turn it off.

March 28, 1992

rain/snow

"Lot of discomfort and then after physical therapy downright pain. Dad stayed long time, after medicine kicked in he left."

I went to physical therapy every day. I was so weak. They did exercises with me that were sometimes painful. It would wear me out.

March 30, 1992

70th day

"This AM *extremely painful long muscle spasms, but okay for muscle relaxants as needed, instead of every eight hours. Sue came up and told Josh about her pet ferret, very interesting to Josh. Going to x-ray Josh's right hip, maybe something pinched."*

I was still in a great deal of pain, due to the muscle spasms, I was constantly fighting them. I was hot and sweaty most of the time. Sue Duffney was a neighbor. I remember her telling me how when she was younger she had a pet ferret, and how she used to take it rabbit hunting. I thought that was pretty neat.

April 3, 1992

40 degrees 10 AM *sunny, "Took Josh outside for twenty minutes after* AM *physical therapy; windy, but he liked it. Roger Marks stopped by at noon to see Josh. Doing good on new muscle relaxant."*

Tuesday, April 7, 1992

"Very attentive and interested in all I share about home and friends. Shakes head no until I get the right radio station for him. Laughed and laughed about Robin story and Bobby DeHare."

Bobby DeHare was my dad's cousin from Michigan. He was famous or more accurately infamous for his practical jokes. Anyway, he had a bet with the people he worked with on the first sighting of a spring robin. I think it was a yearly bet. So what he did was shoot a robin during the previous summer then stuck it in his freezer until the spring. He could then pull it out and win his bet, which he did, not knowing that it was against the law, the robin being the state bird of Michigan.

April 9, 1992

80ᵗʰ day

"Josh going to Sister Kenny rehab—maybe Monday."

Sister Kenny was a rehab hospital, but before I could leave I had to build up my tolerance of sitting up to at least two hours in a wheelchair. At the time of my accident I was about five foot eleven and I weighed

155 to 160 pounds. When I woke from my coma, I found that I was now six foot one. I don't know if I had a growth spurt, or if it was the nutrients in the tube feeding that made me grow. In any case, I was now the tallest person in my family, at about six foot one and a half. I also lost close to 75 pounds, due to sweating along with the constant muscle spasms. The fact that I had no real food to eat for so long didn't help matters either. I was literally skin and bones. I looked like a prison camp survivor; I was no more than a skeleton of my old self. So when they sat me in a wheelchair for the first time, I screamed and cried in pain, because I was sitting directly on my bones. After they figured out what was wrong, they got me a seat cushion for the wheelchair. I still had to build up my tolerance of sitting up for at least 2 hours in the chair before I could be transferred to the Sister Kinney rehab hospital.

April 13, 1992

"Exciting day for Josh—left Crosby at 1 PM, arrived here at Sister Kenny 3:30, getting him settled in nice room on third floor. Dad reading funny book to Josh."

For the second time in my life, I would be taking a ride in an ambulance. It was a three-hour ride to the Twin Cities, where the rehab hospital was located.

April 14, 1992

85ᵗʰ day,

"Josh has had an eventful day—Dr. G. examined him, good report, occupational therapy, physical therapy also, and he is now in speech therapy to see if he can eat and drink here—every hospital different—he is in his second wheelchair of the day and one is on order for him—coming on Friday."

I had a new doctor and I did not care for her too much. I think first impressions are often correct: I thought she was an idiot. I was pretty sick of doctors by this point. I felt like she used me as a guinea pig for her drug trials.

They had a bit of a hard time finding a wheelchair that would fit me. I had lost so much muscle that I would flop over to the side if not propped up.

April 15, 1992

86ᵗʰ day

"Passed swallowing test and can eat everything except popcorn and peanuts. Long day—he was awake the whole time I was there, except for a nap. He mouthed "Mom" and "Dad" and the speech therapist's name "Jo" in speech therapy today."

I still could not talk because of the trake tube in my neck. My first meeting with the speech therapist went okay. She had me mouth

53

some different sounds. When I mouthed the word "shit," she started to laugh.

Thursday AM, *April 16, 1992*

87ʰ day.

"Trake changed to Jackson type this AM. *Walked in and Dr. was feeding him cheerios. Still gets real upset—pain—discomfort. Is off all previous meds. Now going to get something for sweating. Told I should put up posters and stuff to stimulate. So he doesn't regress."*

They took me off most of the drugs, which was good. When I first got there, they had me on all kinds of drugs. They wanted to put me back on Theo-Dur (an asthma drug), but thankfully my mom had enough sense to tell them no. The doctor took me off some pills only to put me on others. That was the doctor's answer for everything; just give him a different pill, and see what happens. I swear that is what she was thinking.

She mistook my pain for anxiety, so I was put on an antidepressant. It didn't do anything except make me sleepy. Meanwhile, I was given something to control my sweating. This came in the form of a shot in my belly once or twice a day. I was told it was "Heparin" (a blood thinner), often used to keep IV sites open; it burns going in. As far as putting posters up, that was sort of pointless, for I could no longer see. People could describe them to me, but it wasn't the same.

Thursday PM, *April 16, 1992*

"Josh got a new trake with plug. Ate turkey and Jell-O for dinner."

They gave me a new trake, this one had a plug at the end of the tube. I was now able to eat more solid foods. The one good thing was that the food at this hospital was much improved. They gave you menu cards that you could fill out to pick your meals for the week. There was also a cafeteria that had all kinds of different types of food. Best of all, the hospital actually had a McDonalds attached to it. I thought that was ironic since people came to this hospital for among other things, to have a heart bypass surgery.

Friday, April 17, 1992

88th day

"Josh and I went outside and stopped at McDonalds for a strawberry milk shake. Taking rest this afternoon. I tried to decorate his room. Got a couple new books for him to hear and another balloon".

To this day, I do not like balloons, Jell-O, or Popsicles, they remind me of the hospital. My mom did her best to decorate my room with cards and posters that my friends and classmates made. They were all get well cards and I could not see them. A few of them were read to me; they didn't do much to cheer me up. They upset me and made me cry instead. After that, they stayed on the wall.

I enjoyed being read to. Before my accident, when I could see, I used to love to read. After the accident, reading helped take my mind off the pain.

Chapter Twelve

Never Give Up

Into the darkness I stumble and fall,

running blindly, away from it all.

The shadows swirl and dance,

In the silvery light of the moon.

I press forward through the darkness and gloom.

I refuse to give up.

I will never give up.

I can't lie down and quit and let the bastards win.

My mind is still here.

My sanity hasn't waned.

It is just so hard starting all over again.

April 18, 1992

4:10PM

"This afternoon Joshua Paul LaRue spoke! He said "Mom, Josh, cheeseburger, shake—strawberry, french fries with ketchup". He also said "hi dad—bye dad" on the phone. Shannon and Joe stopped by. He talked! Good job Josh!"

I had gotten my trake removed the day before, and with the tube out of my neck the hole had healed overnight. I was finally able to speak after long months of frustrating silence. My voice felt and sounded foreign to me after months of disuse, though I couldn't talk more than a croaking whisper. I remember my first few words were of food. I hadn't eaten real food in a few months, and damn I was hungry. Speaking was an effort, after a few words I would grow tired. My words rang crystal clear—like a bell—in my mind, but my speech was now often a bit slurred and hard to understand.

Sunday, April 19, 1992

90th day

"Dad, Jason, Ben, Jed, and I took Josh outside (over 60 degrees) today. Dad is reading canoe story. Ben is coloring a picture for Josh's wall. Jed and Jas went to the car for cards and a poster for Josh. Jack and Deb stopped—he's doing much better. He said both our names. Joked and laughed."

It was a two-and-a-half hour drive to this hospital. My dad would visit as much as he could. They had a hotel connected to the hospital called the Wasie Center. I believe it was free for the patients' family members. It was kind of like the Ronald McDonald house. My mom stayed there most of the time, but occasionally she would spend the night at her aunt's house in Minneapolis or go home for a few days.

Monday, April 20, 1992

91ˢᵗ day

"Lori B. stopped to see you: Josh started to cry a lot, couldn't take it so I left. We all love you and miss you at work. I stopped last Thursday and cried then too. But looks great!"

Lori was one of my aides from the nursing home. I was still in a lot of pain, plus, those stupid pills they had me on made me emotional, and I would cry a lot.

Wednesday, April 22, 1992

"Snow up north. Dad and I arrived at 9:30 AM helped to feed the rest of your breakfast. Your trake hole healed up in one day! Trake tube out Monday, in AM. They are still talking about it today. We had an 11:00 meeting with Dr. G. Josh stays here four—six weeks. New wheelchair today with improvised headrest of foam and duct tape. I am staying at the Wasie Center, nice place."

They tried different wheelchairs for me, but I had lost so much muscle and was so weak that I had a hard time holding my head up. Since there wasn't a chair with a headrest available, my dad improvised a headrest out of some foam and duct tape. That was the first of many wheelchair modifications my dad would make. I have owned six or seven wheelchairs of my own, and my dad has had to help me modify most of them.

April 28, 1992

"Dad came down on Sunday, we went down to McDonald's for lunch. Jack V. came by Saturday eve. Josh was very glad to see him. But the minute Jack left, he looked to me and said 'book'. We finished the Northwood's story and started one about a ten-year-old boy walking down Africa in the 50s. Took Josh outside twice yesterday. Met Bruce E., the paramedic that got air into Josh at the gas station. Told Josh about fishing on the Portage Lake. Josh became so excited as that is where he and Joe have gone. Bruce prayed for Josh. Josh talking more now and very delighted when my lazy ears finally pick up what he is whispering. He relaxes easier now, early morning a little bad yet and leg spasms at night. Kept him up in a chair later, hoping that helped. His spirits on the whole are good and he laughs a lot at me"

I don't know if I believe in fate or coincidence. But in any case, I ended up meeting the man who saved my life. My mom and I were sitting outside, across the street from the hospital, when out of the blue, a man I've never seen strolled up to us, introduced himself, and began talking. I guess he recognized me. I found out his name was Bruce and that his dad was also in the hospital. I believe he said it was a heart attack. That's the reason he was here, he explained. What do you say to someone who has saved your life, someone who has placed his mouth over your cold, lifeless lips? Someone who has pounded on your chest in an attempt to get your stubborn heart to beat? I really didn't know what to say to him. For a time, I wanted to be mad at him for bringing me back. I desperately wanted someone to blame for my problems. If I had someone to blame, then I could understand *the how* and *why* this had to happen to me. But there was no one to point the finger at, no one to blame. That was hard for me to accept and to deal with at first. But I soon realized that thinking that way was not only pointless, but selfish as well.

I did have a chance to meet Bruce one other time. It was about a year later as I was leaving the rehab center in Crosby for one of my tri-weekly physical therapy and speech sessions; I was living at home by then. Anyway, as I was heading out the door I heard someone call my name, and when I looked up, there was Bruce. I spoke to him, well I tried to, but my speech was still not very good at that time. But he understood. I told him *thank you* and he understood.

April 30, 1992

"Going up in the 80's today. Josh and I went out a couple times during the day and an hour last night. Little sunburned. Mr. Kotel, from Brainerd, called today and the kids today are making videos, posters, and cards for Josh. Plus he will graduate. Josh is going swimming this afternoon at 3 PM Dad coming about that time. Almost done with African book and start one on the falcons. They are going to get a talking player for Josh."

Mr. Kotel was the guidance counselor from my high school. It also happened that my friend Noelle worked in the office. I was three credits short from graduation, but he had agreed to overlook those credits. I was told that they would be counted as life-experience credits, for those are the hardest to earn. He was a pretty nice guy, even though I hardly knew him. He let my friends cut class to make a video for me. It was a bunch of them goofing around, playing loud music, and acting stupid. They filmed it from the commons area inside the school. It was pretty funny—it made me laugh and sad at the same time. I missed my friends.

May 4, 1992

"Full schedule today, swimming at the end of it."

My days at the hospital were full of frustration and pain. Starting about 6 AM, Arlie the Amazon woman would do my p.t. range-of-motion exercises. She was about six feet two inches tall and strong. She would bend my tight joints, pulling and stretching my stiff unused limbs. My muscles would burn and scream in protest, often bringing tears to my eyes. I remember one morning, while she was wrenching my right arm straight, I caught my breath from the pain for a moment, long enough to call her a fucking bitch. I was mad. I was sick of her hurting me. She left the room, returning a few minutes later with my mom in tow. She had told on me for what I had said. I didn't care: I was mad. That's not the first time she was called that by a patient. For some reason, I don't know why, my speech was slurred and hard to understand most of the time, but whenever I uttered a swear word, it would come out clear as a bell. Most days I would be worn out from my therapies, physical therapy, occupational therapy, and speech therapy, that I would have to take a nap in the afternoon. They tried to take me into the pool, but I didn't like it. For one thing I was still paralyzed and could not move, that was a bit unsettling. Another thing was that I had zero body fat. And even though they said the pool was heated, I still froze. When I came out of the pool my teeth would be chattering and my lips would be purple from the cold. It was supposed to help my muscle spasms, but I don't think it helped, so after a few times I told them no more.

May 7, 1992

"Happy Birthday Benjamin. Josh slept through the May 6,1992 evening electrical fire at Sister Kenny Abbot North Western hospital. Bad-smelling

smoke, kept his door closed, the air ok in there. Kept his wheelchair by the bed. Josh's arms straightens out really good and he sat up alone yesterday in pt. Spells out words really good, and my lousy ears are getting better."

May 7th was my little brother's birthday. The day before, they had an electrical fire in the poolroom of the hospital. I slept through it, being worn out from the pt. The fire smelled up the place something awful.

I hated p.t.; I was so weak. I was getting stronger so slowly it was hard to tell. One of the things that they would do was sit me up on a raised platform called a mat. Then the p.t. assistants would take turns pushing me over. I felt like a defective Weeble Wobble toy, because I fell over almost every time.

Chapter Thirteen

Don't blink

Sometimes my emotions can get the better of me,

And when the tears stream down my face it's hard to see.

Anger, sorrow, passion and pain:

This life of mine can get rough at times.

I try to be happy; I try not to complain.

I try to be strong; I try not to cry.

But sometimes it just hurts so bad inside.

Sometimes I wish I could forget all the heartache and pain,

To forget about reality for awhile and just go insane.

Yeah this life of mine can get hard at times,

But what the hell am I supposed to do?

I don't have any answers; no, I don't have a clue.

How can I help people? Really, what can I do?

I get angry and frustrated, because I can't do the simple things that

people take for granted.

I have to ask for help with things that I would rather do for myself.

Yeah, this life of mine can be hell at times.

Sometimes I feel like giving up, calling it quits, throwing in the towel,

and saying fuck this shit.

Sometimes it feels like the whole weight of the world is crashing

down upon me.

There's nowhere to turn; I feel hopeless and stuck.

All I can say is for you to try to make the most of each and every day,

Cause in the blink of an eye your whole world could get fucked.

May 11, 1992

112th day

Rain.

"Josh had pain-block shot this morning in his muscles of the right leg. Hopefully this will make a huge difference."

The point I want to make to those of you who are reading this is that doctors don't know everything. Doctors practice medicine. It's my opinion that most of them will never get it right, thus the term *doctor's practice*. And who do doctors practice on? Well, their patients, of course. Now I am not trying to knock the medical profession. I have known some good doctors and nurses in my life. But I did not care for Dr. G., nor did I have confidence in her. May 11th was my baby brother's birthday. That was also the morning the doctor administered the motor point block shots in my right leg. I had gotten contractures from my time in the nursing home, from lying around so long without exercise. A contracture occurs when a muscle shrinks, and the tendon becomes shortened, contracting the joint like a shrinking rubber band. Contractures are painful. They can sometimes be relieved with range-of-motion and splints or braces to stretch out the shortened tendons. Other times, surgery is needed to correct the problem. I had a severe contracture of my right leg. My knee was bent frozen at nearly a ninety-degree angle. My right arm was contracted at the elbow, and so were both of my wrists. The doctor explained the procedure to my mom, who in turn explained it to me. It would consist of a series of shots into the muscles of my right leg. The shots were supposed to loosen the muscles to help with the pain of the contracture. I had had hundreds of shots before, so what could a few more hurt? That's what I thought at the time.

I soon found out how wrong I was. The morning I had the shots, the doctor entered the room followed by three nurses, two of whom were male nurses. I figured out too late that their job was to hold me down. Looking back, I thought if I had been stronger at the time, I would have seriously hurt some of them. The nurses gathered around my hospital bed. Two of them each took an arm and the third practically sat on my legs, for they knew what was coming, but I still didn't have a clue. The doctor filled a long syringe with Phenobarbital. Then, after wiping my leg with alcohol swabs, she began to inject me with the medicine. Now the needle that she was using for this procedure was not only long, but was also connected to some kind of electrode or electric current. It was not an ordinary syringe. As she sank the needle deeper into my flesh and muscle, I could feel the medicine start to burn. That's when the doctor turned on the electrode to the needle. The pain was instant and severe. I gritted my teeth together; it didn't help. I could feel my muscles spasm and contract with each pulse of electric current. My back arched, and I began to howl and shriek in pain. I fought to get free, but the nurses held me pinned to the bed. I felt like I was being electrocuted from the inside out. I believe she gave me three injections: two in my thigh, and one in my calf muscle. I was crying in pain, yelling and pleading for her to stop, but she wouldn't. I even tried cursing at her. **I called her every awful, vile name I could think of.** But it was no use. She just ignored me. When it was all over I lay panting, soaked in sweat, whimpering, spent, and exhausted on my hospital bed. The worst part was that it was all for nothing. The shots did not help. I would later have to have surgery on my leg in order to fix the problem.

Chapter Fourteen

Ocean

As the oceans of time swell and surge in my mind.

I am cast into a troubled sea.

I choke, gasping for breath.

As a flood of memories threaten to drown me.

My black soul floats upon the tide, like a cork.

Longing for the shelter of the harbor and the safety of the

port.

I have been a drift on these troubled waters for such a

long time.

Riding out the storm of anger that rages in my mind.

There I was: seventeen years old and stuck in the hospital for God knew how long. It gave me a long time to think. It gave me some comfort to know that I was not the only person going through rehab. My room was on the third floor, halfway down the hall. To the right was the nurse's station, and to the far left, at the end of the hall, was a bank of elevators. Across the hall was a small dining room, and a little further down the hall was the shower room. I also think that past the nurse's station there was a room with padded walls. The residents on the third floor were mostly comprised of head injuries.

The winter of 1992 was very snowy. There were two or three people on my floor who were in accidents involving snowplows. There was a kid about my age named Patrick. I believe he was from somewhere in southern Minnesota. Apparently, he was on a snowmobile when he got hit by a snowplow truck. I don't know if he was attempting to cross the road or what. In any case, he ended up with me on the third floor. There was also a guy about twenty-one or twenty-two named Brian. I think he was in a car accident. Then there was Darla; I believe a snowplow hit her pickup and that's how she ended up on the third floor. Darla was something else. Every five minutes she would be pushing the nurse call button and yelling down the hall that she had to pee. But I also think she spoke for all of us, for whenever anyone asked her how she was or how she was feeling, she would always give them the same answer: "I've been better."

Getting a shower in the shower room sucked. They would wheel this gurney into my room, and then two nurses would slide my naked body onto it. Then they would cover me with a sheet and push me down the hall to the shower room. The gurney was very hard and painful to lie on. I had no fat or meat to offer any padding. My body was basically a sack of skin and bones and the gurney felt like a sheet of hard plywood under me. Once in the shower room, the nurses would then literally hose me down with the showerhead. I remember one time when the nurses were giving Brian a shower. He somehow managed to get ahold of the showerhead from one of the nurses. Then he proceeded to spray both of them, soaking them both from head to foot. I found that to be quite funny. After awhile, I was able to shower sitting up in a shower chair, in my own bathroom. That was somewhat better.

The nurses and therapists at this hospital were, for the most part, pretty decent. There was Mary Kay, who was funny, and I think also my favorite. There was Beth, who was a few years older than me. She drove a Honda CRX and always made sure my radio was on the right channel. There was Carol, who had a black lab named Josh that she brought to the hospital once so I could see him. There was Denise, who was good at shaving and also the best at brushing teeth. When you can no longer take care of yourself, personal hygiene becomes important. There was Noreen, who was always there if I had a problem. There was KJ; he was a cool guy. It was nice to talk to a guy once in awhile. There were two older nurses who had been there forever; their names were Dot and Kay. One of them had even met Mother Teresa once. There was another male nurse who worked there named Shane that I didn't care for. He reeked as though he bathed in cheap aftershave. Often his smell would precede him, and you could also smell him long after he left the room. I didn't like him, he gave me the creeps. My first night there he came into my room and started touching my hair. He ran his fingers through my hair a few times and told me that I had such nice, pretty, curly hair. I could not move or talk, nor could I see. I was mad and also scared. I could not cry for help; all I could do was shake my head and glare up at him. It is an awful feeling to be helpless and vulnerable.

That guy was weird; I didn't want him near me or taking care of me. The whole time I was there, I never once asked him to help me. I did my best to avoid him, and didn't speak to him. I think he got the hint, because he left me alone after that.

The therapists at the hospital were also pretty decent, except for Arlie the Amazon, who could be a little rough at times. For the most part, the rest of the therapists were okay. There was Jill in physical therapy. She was a tiny little woman, who stood about five feet nothing. But as small as she was, she could pick people up and move them around like nothing; she was pretty amazing. There was Julie in occupational therapy; she worked with my arms and hands, trying to get them to work. She would tell me dirty jokes to make me laugh and take my mind off the pain. She was pretty cool. My speech therapist was named Jo-Ellen. She was a busy lady, so I often saw her assistant. I believe her name was Jenny.

I hated being cooped up inside the hospital. I tried to get outside as much as possible. There I could listen to the birds, and hear the wind rustle through the trees, and feel the warm sun on my upturned face. For a few brief moments, I could forget where I was and all that had happened. When the weather was nice, I would sometimes talk my speech therapist into pushing me outside. There was a small deck on the second floor. I would often sit out there and sometimes have my speech lessons out there as well. It beat being stuck in some cramped, stuffy office for an hour.

Learning to talk again was one of the most difficult and frustrating things that I ever had to do. I knew what I wanted to say. I could picture the words and sentences in my mind clearly, but when I tried to talk my speech was often hard to understand and sometimes slurred, as if I were drunk. My tongue didn't seem to want to cooperate with my brain. I would have to retrain both of them. To this day, I am still very soft-spoken and have trouble getting certain words out. It still frustrates me.

I was slowly regaining some movement and getting stronger. I was now able to scratch my own nose. It may not sound like much to some people, but it was a big deal to me. No longer would I be dependent on others for everything. Finally, here was something small I could do for myself! The thing that people reading this need to understand is that physical therapy is very hard and often painful. Also, the person has to really want to get better for it to work. That's the only way it will really work. Every day I went to physical therapy, occupational therapy, and sometimes speech therapy. In occupational therapy, they were working on fashioning a squirt gun that I could use. It might sound silly, but I was motivated. A chance to squirt my little brothers with a squirt gun? Hell yes! I was motivated. They helped me to work on other tasks as well, like pushing buttons and grabbing things.

I had had a meeting with the doctor a few weeks before to talk about goals. My mom was there along with a couple of the nurses. I told the doctor that my one goal was to graduate with my class. In occupational therapy, they started working with me on reaching my hand and arm up so I could grab hold and accept my diploma.

Most of the patients' rooms at the hospital were decorated with get-well cards and pictures and posters from home. Patrick had an FFA banner on his wall that his classmates had made for him. FFA stands for Future Farmers of America. The walls in my room were also covered with cards from my friends and classmates, but I could not see them, nor could I read them. I wanted something from home, something I could touch and feel and even hold on to. I asked my mom if my dad could get it for me. On his next visit he brought it, my kayak paddle.

I guess my dad got some funny looks walking into the hospital with a nine-foot-long paddle over his shoulder. He propped it up in the corner of my room. All the nurses wanted to know what the heck it was. I was probably the only person in the state with a kayak paddle in his hospital room, but I didn't care.

Monday May 18, 1992

"Dad, Aimee, Ben, and Jed were here yesterday. Josh was up eight hours in his wheelchair, comfortable. No hand spasms all weekend because no air splints. Talked Saturday AM about his accident and yesterday asked about his jacket. Wonderful memory he has. Josh told me Saturday, I don't have asthma anymore."

My brothers and sister came to visit the day before. I had had a bad day, and my sister got upset. She couldn't take it. She left the room crying, and I don't blame her. The problem was the tens unit that physical therapy had ordered for me. It was supposed to be placed on my back to relieve the muscle spasms. A tens unit is a small device, about the size of two packs of cards with a battery pack and long, trailing wires. Connected to these wires were flat sticky electrodes, the kind they use on EKG machines, I think. The purpose of the device is to conduct a small electric current into one's muscles in order to relieve pain.

All I knew was that I hated it! There was also a dial to adjust the intensity of the electric current to the electrodes. Apparently, the nurse's aide who placed the unit on my back was unfamiliar with it. She didn't know what she was doing, because before leaving the room and shutting the door behind her, she cranked the dial up as high as it would go. When my family walked in some time later, I was hysterical: crying, screaming, and thrashing around in bed. Trying, without success, to distance myself from the electrodes that were stuck on my back. It was not a good day. To quote Darla: "I've been better!"

Lying around day after day in the hospital gave me plenty of time to think. At first, I didn't know how bad-off I was. I knew that I was weak. I remember picturing myself running up and down a flight of stairs to strengthen my muscles. I could imagine it clearly in my mind's eye, but it would remain as only a fantasy. For in truth, it would be two more years of rehab before I would ever walk again.

My mom was a bit of a religious person. I think she thought I would have a miraculous recovery and get up and walk out of the hospital. I don't know, maybe it gave her some hope. But I soon came to realize the gravity of my situation. All the prayers in the world weren't going to help me now. I remember thinking to myself, "what the hell am I going to do now?" Over and over in my mind, the same thought kept repeating itself, "what the hell am I going to do now?" I didn't have a clue, nor an answer.

Meanwhile, the nurses told me that Patrick and Darla were learning to walk. I still had my mind though. Thankfully, the accident had spared that much, at least. I had my mind and my super-acute hearing. That's all I had to work with at that time. The rest of my body didn't seem to want to work. I was blind, I could hardly talk, and I could not walk or use my hands. I remember thinking about Helen Keller. Maybe because she was the only blind person I could think of. She was blind, mute, and also deaf. But she could walk and use her hands! I didn't want to compare myself to her, but I did. I didn't want to be worse off than Helen Keller!

That day I talked to my mom about the accident, I sat up in my wheelchair and asked her to bring me my paddle. I sat there as she laid it across my lap, and helped me wrap my hands around it. It felt good to hold my paddle in my hands once again. It felt comfortable.

My hands were once calloused and strong from hours of paddling, but now they lay useless and weak as I gripped my paddle. I had lost everything in the blink of an eye. My whole world had turned upside down, and I had to face the hard truth that I might not ever get better. That day I talked to my mom about my accident. I asked her if she knew what happened, and she told me. It was different hearing it from her point of view.

She arrived at the hospital after I had died, and after the paramedics had brought me back. But unfortunately, I would remember, about that morning, everything until I passed out and took my last breath. I also knew something that my mom didn't; it was the cruelest of ironies. I no longer had asthma. I told her and she was happy saying *praise Jesus* and so forth. As for me I was furious. It was if a black cloud of anger and hate had settled over me. I had never felt so angry in my entire life. It was like a white-hot flame burning in my brain. Later that night, as I lay crying in my bed, I cursed God. I damned him to hell for letting this happen to me. What kind of God would do such a thing as to cure my asthma, only to leave me a cripple for life? If that was the price I had to pay to rid myself of asthma, then I would gladly have my asthma back. I used to wish for anything not to have asthma. I guess I should have been more careful what I wished for. I was miserable laying there feeling sorry for myself. I wanted to die. I prayed for death. I am not a religious person, but that night I prayed. I prayed to God to let me die. But since I had already damned God, he wasn't going to listen. I never felt so helpless and alone in my life. I felt cheated somehow and I wanted my life back. I wanted my body back as well. I was mad. It wasn't fair! I was a good person; I never hurt anyone. Why did this have to happen to me? Why me? With my rage spent, I fell asleep thinking these thoughts. That night would be a turning point in my life. For, in the morning I vowed to never to feel sorry for myself again.

Chapter Fifteen

Defining Moments

The Defining Moment.

There are many defining moments in a man's life.

The secret is being able to notice them when they come

along.

Hindsight is 20/20.

Don't miss the boat, don't take too long.

The choices we make, shape our lives

The paths we take may be narrow or wide.

The things we say and the things we do,

Will someday come back to haunt you.

May 28, 1992

I was allowed to leave the hospital for twenty-four hours, so that I could go home to graduate from high school. The nurses showed my dad how to attach and empty my catheter. I was still in pretty bad shape—it was only a few months before when I had laid at Death's door in a deep coma. Now I was actually going to graduate. I was determined; it was something I felt I had to do, even if I was crippled in a wheelchair. I wasn't going to waste twelve years of education: I had worked too hard to just quit and throw it all away. I was going to finish and graduate with my class. After loading my big cumbersome wheelchair into the trunk, my mom, dad, brother, and I all headed for home.

Once home my dad and brother maneuvered my wheelchair into the kitchen. It felt different to be home. So much had happened; so much had changed. It was hard for me to take it all in. I sat there looking around, trying to make things out. To my right I could hear the hum of the refrigerator. Upon hearing that, it suddenly occurred to me that I felt hungry. I asked my dad if I could have something to eat. When he asked me what I wanted, I told him I didn't care. So he opened the fridge and started naming things. I settled on a half container of coleslaw. That was the first meal I'd had at home in nearly five months.

After I was done eating, my dad pushed me outside. It was a beautiful day, even though I couldn't see. I could still tell the sun was warm on my face and arms, the birds were singing, and under my tires I could smell fresh-cut grass. It smelled good. My dad decided to push me down to the lake, which was about a hundred yards from the back of the house. It was a bumpy ride over the lawn, with cool shadows from the giant shade trees occasionally spaced throughout the yard. I would pass under sun then shade, then sun, then shade again and again on my way to the lake. There was a small grass-covered hill leading from the lawn down to the shore of the lake. My dad parked my chair atop the hill, under the shade of an old twisted willow tree. Then walking down to the shore my dad picked up several big rocks, turning back to me he yelled "Are you ready!?" Up on the bank, I had no idea what he was doing. That's when I heard the big splash, and I started laughing. He was chucking rocks into the lake so I could hear them. They made a superb sound: a big kerplunk followed by a splash. I thought it sounded beautiful. I could have sat there all day atop the hill listening to the seagulls cry, with the smell of the lake in my nostrils. I missed it all so much.

Later that day, my friend Ryan came over, bringing with him my cap and gown. He brought them over so I could have them to wear that night. Also, my friend Joe and his girlfriend Shannon came over to see me. I also remember that my friend Matt was there, along with some others—how many I'm not sure. I was lying down on a pullout couch in the playroom. They all gathered around my bed and told me how happy they were to see me and how good I looked. The last part was probably bullshit. I'm sure I was looking pretty rough. Soon it was time to leave. My mom helped me put on my gown, and then my dad and brothers helped me into the car. It was a beautiful, perfect, May evening. There was no rain in the forecast, so the graduation would take place outside on the football field. It was a twenty-minute drive to the city of Brainerd where I went to school. After parking in the lot and getting me into my wheelchair, my dad and brother pushed me through the gap in the fence onto the running track that circled the football field. I think my mom followed behind with my mortarboard hat. To my left were bleachers full of people, and to the right were hundreds of folding chairs arranged on the football field. Passing by the bleachers, I heard people call out my name. I thought I heard my friend Joe's mom and little sister, my friend Sara, and my boss and his wife. About halfway down the field my family parked my chair. Then finding room on some folding chairs my family sat down behind me.

The ceremony began soon after my mom placed my cap on my head. I remember there was some music and singing along with several speeches by the valedictorian and the class president. There was a kid named Eric, everyone called him Hopper, who gave a speech; about what, I can't remember. When he mentioned a party spot called "Nowhere," the whole class cheered. The joke was that if someone asked you where you were or where you had been, you would say "nowhere." I think a lot of kids got drunk at "Nowhere." Soon the principal, Mr. Hunt, began to recite the names of my classmates. He read them off in alphabetical order, with friends, family, and classmates clapping and cheering after most of the names. Soon they would come to my name I thought, but just then my friends Ryan and Mike appeared at my sides, and before I knew what was happening, I was pushed ahead through the rows of chairs where my classmates sat. When the principal finally called my name, something unexpected and crazy happened. Every person who was there rose to their feet and started to clap and cheer. My 300 or more classmates who were standing behind me and the thousand or so who were sitting on the bleachers were now on their feet, cheering for me. For a brief moment, I didn't know what was going on. Then it dawned on me, and my face split into a huge smile that stayed with me the rest of the night. As I was wheeled up to the podium, I reached out my hand as high and as far as I could and the principal shook it. Then before I could raise my hand again to accept my diploma, the principle laid my diploma in my lap. The people remained on their feet clapping and cheering the whole way back to where my family was sitting. The noise was deafening. I never knew I had so many friends.

As I sat there on the side of the track, I was still a little in shock. I could not believe so many people knew who I was, or for that matter would care enough to give me a standing ovation. It was the nicest thing anyone has ever done for me. Soon, the last of the names were called. There was a cheer as some of my classmates threw their caps in the air, and then it was over. Families began streaming off the bleachers and onto the football field. Cameras flashed as hundreds of hugs were exchanged. There were masses of people everywhere. Their loud, excited voices surrounded me from all sides. Soon it was time to go. My dad began pushing my chair through the sea of people back towards the car. His progress was slowed somewhat by my friends wishing me congratulations and by the girls who were giving me kisses. I got a lot of kisses that night. My nurse Lori, from the nursing home, was there, I think she gave me six or seven kisses. After taking a mountain of pictures, everybody said their good-byes and then it was time to leave. As my dad was loading my chair into the trunk of the car, I remember my grade school teacher, Mrs. Claxton, stuck her head in the passenger-side window to talk to me. I remember she told me that she was proud of me. I wasn't sure, but I think she may have been crying. After that, we all headed for home and the next day I returned to the hospital.

Chapter Sixteen

Blind Boy

It has been said that blindness is a curse.

Blindness is a disease.

I have to admit, sometimes I miss using these eyes of

mine.

It is a visual world.

Most everything nowadays revolves around sight,

But I get buy.

I can still read and write.

My books may not have pages.

So what, I can still type.

It is just a little tough.

I get around from place to place.

I don't use a dog and I don't use no cane.

I just remember where I have been, so I can make it home

again.

I cannot see peoples' faces.

But if I know you, I can always tell:

By the sound of your voice,

The way you walk,

Or the way you smell.

Back at the hospital, I continued to go to my different therapies. In physical therapy, they asked me how my graduation had gone. They were impressed when they found out that the foot pedal to my wheelchair had fallen off on the way to the podium. So I had to hold my leg up in order to keep my foot from being run over by the wheelchair. I held my foot up the whole way to and from the podium.

In occupational therapy, they were anxious to know if I was able to grasp my diploma from the principal's hands, since that's what they had been working with me on. I told them I tried to, but when I raised my hand up to take it, the principal shook it instead. I didn't have a chance! The principal just laid it in my lap for me. In truth, I think that was probably the best solution, for I may have dropped it instead.

A few days later, as I was sitting outside, something curious happened. I was sitting there with my mom, listening to the birds that were flocking around a man's feet. He had been feeding them french fries from a McDonald's bag. No doubt with a McDonald's in the hospital, all the birds in the neighborhood ate well. Anyway, while I was sitting there, I happened to look down and when I did so I saw something that caught my eye. It was a fuzzy patch of florescent yellow. It took me a minute to realize what I was looking at. It was the yellow-painted curb of the hospital's front parking lot. It was just a small glimpse of color, very blurry and out of focus, but I could see it.

Up to this time, I wasn't able to see much of anything. My vision was very poor. Everything was fuzzy. People and objects all looked like dark shadows to me. It was very difficult to distinguish things or make them out. I compensated by memorizing little things like sounds and smells. I don't know if that's something all blind people do or not, but it was something that I was able to do fairly easily. I would listen to sounds and after identifying them I would then commit them to my memory. I could tell who was at the nurse's station by the sound of their voices, or who was walking down the hall by the noise of their shoes. Or even who was entering my room by the way they knocked. I knew which nurses smoked by the smell on their clothes. By the sounds and smells I could also tell where I was at in the hospital. Up until this point I wasn't able to see colors, but now, apparently, I was.

A few days later my dad came down to visit. I remember he was pushing my chair down the first-floor hall. I think we were going outside. As we passed by the chapel, I yelled for him to stop. There was a small chapel in the hospital where I think they held Sunday church services sometimes. It was a quiet place where people could be alone; to pray or to grieve, or whatever the case may be. The reason I asked my dad to stop was that I saw something through the chapel door. There were stained glass windows inside, that I had not noticed before. I remember telling my parents that I could see the colors. Everything still looked fuzzy and unfocused to my blind eyes. I sat there for a long time gazing up at the colors; I thought they were beautiful.

I was still getting better, although it was at a snail's pace. I was taken off the catheter and now was able to use the bathroom sitting up on a commode chair. Before that, I was made to wear adult diapers. It was humiliating. After my accident, I had to relearn many things and going to the bathroom was one of them. Fortunately, my potty training went a lot faster the second time around.

I was still going to my different therapies. The therapists did what they could to help. But I was still in pretty rough shape. I didn't want to be there. I was seventeen; I should have been going to parties with my friends, but now everything had changed. It was time for me to grow up. Nevertheless, I had recovered enough to be sent home. So a couple weeks later, I said my good-byes to the nurses, loaded up the car with my new commode/shower chair in the trunk, and headed for home. It was almost six months to the day of my accident when I was released from the hospital and was allowed to gohome.

Chapter Seventeen

Help Me

I need help every day.

With simple ordinary things, that most people take for granted.

I appreciate the help.

But I would much rather do things for myself.

Not being able to help myself is very frustrating, and so very hard.

I get pissed off sometimes, when my words won't come out right.

And I end up sounding like a retard.

I have no more modesty.

No more class, I am a grown man.

Who needs help taking a shower,

and with wiping my ass.

It's humiliating being so helpless.

It's so hard to communicate.

It is maddening to want to do things.

But my body won't cooperate.

O, God help me.

June 20, 1992

I believe it was Thomas Wolf who wrote you can't go home again. I have never heard truer words spoken. I could not just pick the threads of my old life back up and start over where I left off. So much had happened, and I had lost so much for that to ever be possible. I was not afraid of challenges, but the obstacles that were facing me seemed very overwhelming to me at the time. I had three different disabilities that I was going to have to overcome. It was going to be hard enough trying to deal with one problem, but my situation was compounded and made worse by my multiple disabilities. I had lost the use of my hands and the ability to walk. I was now blind, having lost nearly all of my vision. My speech was affected as well, making it very difficult to speak or to be understood. I felt very useless and helpless.

Arriving home and pulling up to the house, my brothers were outside waiting for me. They were on the cement patio, taking turns practicing riding wheelies in my new wheelchair. The medical supply people had delivered the wheelchair along with a hospital bed earlier that day. My dad had converted my little brothers' room into my room, and they both moved upstairs. In addition to setting up my hospital bed, my dad had also remodeled the bathroom that was outside my new room. He tore out the old shower stall and built a roll-in shower for me. He was very handy when it came to designing and building things.

The first week I was home my mom hardly left me alone. I think she was happy that I was finally home, because she spoiled me a little bit. I remember she bought me Cocoa Krispies for breakfast because I told her that's what I wanted. The funny thing was that, growing up, my mom would never buy sugared cereal for us kids. I remember when I was ten I pedaled my bike up to the gas station, over a mile away, to buy a box of Captain Crunch with my own money, which I took home and hid in my room. The next morning I proudly poured a bowl of my very own box of cereal. My mom saw me and got very mad. She wanted to know what I thought I was doing. I tried to tell her that it was my box of cereal, that I had bought with my own money. She would hear none of it. She said, "That may be your cereal, but it's my milk in the fridge." After that, I had to share the rest of the box with my brothers until it was empty. She taught me not to be selfish.

All the time I had spent in the hospital was hard on my family. Nobody wants to see their son or brother get hurt and end up in that kind of situation. It was particularly hard for my dad to deal with. Now I was home and there would be new challenges and stresses to deal with. One of the first things I did after arriving home, was I had my mom throw out all my old asthma medicine. I no longer had asthma. I didn't want to be reminded of it, nor did I want to be dependent on it any more. Between my nebulizer machine, ampoules of drugs, and bottles of saline, along with all the bottles of pills and the two or three different types of inhalers, she managed to fill two large trash bags. She also (after discussing it with my dad) threw away all of the stupid antidepressants that the doctor prescribed for me. I wasn't depressed. Perhaps frustrated and a bit pissed off in the beginning, but I wasn't depressed. I did not want to be dependent on pills. Plus, those antidepressants made me feel like a damn zombie, so much so that one night I fell out of my hospital bed and had no memory of it the next morning. After that, my parents took me off the pills.

Chapter Eighteen

The Lake

There is a lake.

It's in my dreams,

Shrouded in memory,

From days long past.

It's where I learned to fish.

It's where I learned to swim,

And to float on my back.

It's where I learned to ice-skate along the frozen shore.

It's where my brothers and I raced to,

Running out the door.

There was a small island near the eastern shore.

It's where we built a fort as kids.

It's where we played pirate,

And where we played war.

We had to abandon that fort reluctantly,

When we found out that the whole island

Was covered in poison ivy.

A whole week went past,

Where we found ourselves covered in an itchy rash.

When evening came,

The shadows would grow long behind the pines.

The wind would die,

And the surface of the lake would become as smooth as glass.

Soon there would be hundreds of tiny ripples to see,

Like falling rain,

Dimpling the surface

As the fish would rise to feed.

The sun would slowly sink behind the hills,

The heavens would glow,

Painting the evening sky.

It would be reflected off the water,

So it looked like there were two sunsets in the sky.

Some days it would be windy,

And the whitecaps would crash upon the beach.

The dead fish would be washed ashore,

Smelling pungent and sweet.

The breaking waves would pile the foam upon the shore

Like mountains of soap suds,

Covering everything in white.

Often the lily pad roots would wash in

Looking like giant turds.

It was a gruesome sight.

Sometimes I still dream of the lake

Late at night.

I dream I can hear the cry of the gulls

As I lay still,

With my eyes closed.

And breathing deep,

I imagine that I still have the scent of the lake in my nose.

My parents were not able to care for me solely by themselves. My dad worked during the week; also at that time it took two people to transfer me in and out of my wheelchair. They needed help caring for me at home. So they contacted a home care agency. (Note to reader, for legal reasons, I have changed the names of the home care companies in this book.) They sent a nurse from the agency to meet with my mom and to evaluate me for home care services. Home health care is a service that provides nurses or nurse's aides to care for someone in their own home, opposed to a nursing home or someplace else. There are different types of home care as well. There is hospice care for people who are terminally ill. There are live-in care attendants and there are also independent providers to name a few. Anyway, the name of the company that the nurse was from was called *Friendly Neighbor* I believe her name was Marilyn. Each home care agency is different; each has its own rules and regulations on how they do things, even how they classify their patients. Friendly Neighbor's system, at that time, used a series of letters to assign to each patient according to the difficulty of care. I remember I was given a letter J to signify the level of care I would need. This was close to the bottom of the barrel, as far as their system went. I think the only letter left was K. I felt sorry for those poor bastards who were classified as the letter K. At least I knew that I wasn't as bad off as some people. Things could be worse. I guess that was something to be thankful for.

After filling out all the forms, I was approved for something like six hours of home care a day. That would include bathing, dressing, oral hygiene, transferring me in and out of bed, feeding me, helping me use the bathroom, and other things to get me ready for the day. My first experience with home care was kind of rough. The girl they sent to take care of me was a big moose of a woman. At first I thought she was a guy. She had horrible personal hygiene; she smelled pretty awful, and I didn't care for her very much. I don't think she liked her job or me much either. I don't remember her name, but what I do remember about her, besides being big and smelly, was when she would help me get dressed, she would pull my underwear up so high and so hard that they would rip. She actually pulled the elastic out of two pairs, ruining them. There's nothing like getting a wedgie first thing in the morning. Shit.

It was hard for me to adjust to everything at home. I was happy to be home where things were familiar, but at the same time everything was now different and nothing would ever be the same. It took awhile to get used to receiving home care. When a person receives home care, they are basically allowing strangers into their home. Now it is the job of the home care agency to screen and do background checks on their employees, and also to train them to do their jobs safely and properly. But sadly, that is not always the case. Sometimes the people they hire can be dishonest. Having to trust strangers in and out of one's home can be stressful. I didn't really have any other choice but to accept the

99

help. That stinky girl ended up leaving and things got better for a time. They sent me a new girl; her name was Maryann. She was in her mid 40s, or so I think, and was very nice.

I may have been blind and stuck in a wheelchair, but I tell you my mind was always going. I was constantly thinking and trying to problem-solve. I was going to have to figure out different ways of doing things, not only to try to improve my situation, but to try to do some of the things I used to love. One of which was fishing. After the accident, I wasn't able to hold on and grasp a fishing pole in my hands, nor was I able to cast or work a reel. I had been fishing since I was three years old, and I wasn't about to quit. In the past I had caught fish in many different ways. I had caught them on a fly rod, on a spinning reel, and by spearing them through a hole in the ice. I had shot fish with my bow, where the arrow is connected to a line. I had caught fish in nets, and also by using my bare hands, but to attempt fishing in my current condition was going to take some thought. Also, how was I going to get my chair up the sandy beach that was in front of the dock? Going down the hill to the dock wouldn't be a problem, because gravity would do most of the work: trying to push my wheelchair tires uphill through loose sand would be the problem. These were some of the problems I had to overcome before I could attempt fishing.   The solutions to both of these problems turned out to be very simple once I thought about it.

When I was three years old, my dad took my brother, who was four at the time, and I fishing for the first time with a coffee can full of worms freshly exhumed from behind the garage. My brother and I with fishing poles in hand raced down to the dock. This was the very same dock where my wheelchair now sat. My dad once again had a coffee can full of worms that he had dug up from behind the garage. In place of the fishing pole, I had my dad tie a fishing line around my wrist. Then after baiting the hook with a worm, he threw the line, bobber and all, off the side of the dock and into the water. It didn't take long before I had a hungry sunfish on the end of my line. When the bobber went under my dad yelled, "jerk". So by jerking my arm up to set the hook, I had caught my first fish since the accident. I didn't care if it was just a sunfish: the fact that I caught it myself felt good. All in all, I would have to say that things went better than the very first time I went fishing. That time I was three years old and my brother and I were anxious to try out our new fishing poles. Racing on to the dock, I waited impatiently for my dad to bait my hook. Stepping to the very end of the dock, I cast my hook and little bobber into the water. When nothing immediately happened, I grew bored and distracted. As I turned to watch my brother get a bite, just then there was a sharp tug on the end of my arm. That's when I lost my balance stumbling backwards off the dock and into the lake. When my dad pulled me out, I was soaking wet and crying, but

I still held tightly to my pole, and on the end of my line there dangled a tiny sun fish. That's how I became a fisherman.

The hand line worked pretty well, I thought. After I had caught a stringer-full with the hand line, my dad and brother then helped me get my chair up the hill. First, they tied one end of a long rope to the front of my chair, and then they tied the other end to the riding mower that was parked atop the hill. Then, with my brother driving and my dad walking behind me to steer, they slowly pulled my chair through the sand and up the hill. It was slick being towed up the hill, and it was kind of fun, too. My dad cleaned and cooked my catch for me. Frying up my freshly caught sunfish made that meal one of the best I ever ate.

Later, I tried to improve on the fish-catching process. With money I got for my birthday, I purchased an automatic fly-fishing reel and a spool of fly line. My idea was to mount the reel to my fishing pole. This particular reel had a recoil spring built into it. As the line was pulled out, the spring inside the reel would wind up and tighten. Then all I had to do was hit a button and the line would be automatically retrieved, so I could reel in a fish without using my hands. I thought it was a good idea and in theory it should have worked. What I didn't count on was the reel working so well. Apparently the reel was designed to help land-fighting salmon and trout, not a little one-ounce sunfish. I remember my brother helped me try it out for the first time. After playing out the line and putting the hook and bobber in the water, he then propped the pole against my chair where I could reach the button. As soon as he told me the bobber was down, I hit the button. Immediately the powerful coiled spring inside the reel sprang to life, zipping up the slack in the line in an instant. It all happened so fast, and the spring was so strong that it cracked my bobber when it was sucked up to the end of my pole.

Chapter Nineteen

Scars

We all carry scars from our past,

Visible reminders of life.

Marks that will follow us forever,

Until the day we pass.

Be it from war,

And its multitude of ways to tear your flesh.

Be it from accidents,

Such as a car crash,

Or be it from surgery

That you have went through in the past.

Some people wear their scars proudly,

Like a badge of courage,

Showing them off for the world to see,

Like a souvenir tattooed upon the skin,

While others prefer to conceal them from prying eyes

from within.

Scars are nothing more than wounds that have healed,

Closing the flesh, no longer able to bleed.

Though not visible, some scars are so painful

That they will never heal,

No matter how old.

These are scars that have been inflicted upon one's heart

Or one's soul.

In addition to Mary Ann, the home care agency sent a younger guy to take care of me. He was twenty-one or twenty-two and his name was Sergey. He was okay, though he didn't do much. What I remember the most about him was that the boy could eat. One night, while my mom was at church, my dad invited him to stay for dinner along with our friend Scotty. Growing up, we often had friends over for dinner or to spend the night. My dad was making pancakes. It was one of his specialties, because it fed a lot of people. Sitting around the table were three of my five brothers, our friend Scotty, my home health aide Sergey and me. My dad was using his big electric griddle to cook on. He could make six pancakes at once on it. Even so, he had a hard time catching up to all of us. After a few pancakes I was full, but everyone else was still going strong. It soon turned into an eating contest. I knew my brothers could eat a lot and Scotty may have been a scrawny kid, but he was also a bottomless pit when it came to food. It soon became apparent though that none of them could keep up with Sergey. Even Scotty, flabbergasted, no longer able to contain himself, exclaimed "Dang boy! What are you, a Somalian?" With that, we all lost it.

A few days later Sergey was working once again. After getting me up in my chair and ready for the day, my mom told Sergey that she was going shopping and would be back in a few hours. She told him that if he got hungry he could help himself, indicating the muffins and the bowl of fruit that sat on the counter. After he gave me lunch, Sergey decided to get something to eat as well. He ate two of the muffins, but I guess he was still hungry because he started pulling food out of the freezer and shoving it in the microwave. After polishing off a whole box of egg rolls, he ate two stuffed chicken meals, followed by a half of a container of chocolate ice cream. When I told him my mom would be mad if he ate all of her ice cream, he told me "Don't worry about it." Needless to say, Sergey sort of ate himself out of a job. Later that night, my mom got quite upset when she discovered he had eaten all the food that she had bought for my lunches, finding all the empty boxes and the wrappers in the trash.

The next person the home care agency sent to take care of me was a girl named Missy. After that, things got better. She was about five years older than me. It turned out, that not only did I graduate in the same class with her little brother, but we knew some of the same people, which was cool. She ended up being my primary care giver, working almost the entire year I lived at home. Hardheaded and intelligent, my whole family liked her. One of the reasons was that she didn't take any of my shit. She made sure that if I was willing to dish it out, I had better be willing to take it. I remember one time, I mouthed off to her about something, and she threatened to take me outside and dump me in a snow bank. I must have said something taunting like "try it," which turned out to be a big mistake. The next thing I knew she had picked me up in a fireman's carry over her shoulder and headed for the front door.

Stepping outside, I remember thinking to myself, "holy shit, this girl is serious!" That's when I started to apologize in earnest. After spinning me around a few times over a particularly deep snow drift, she marched me back inside and flopped me unceremoniously onto my bed. I might add this provided a great deal of amusement and delight for my younger brothers, who were privy to the whole show.

During that summer, I began to receive some speech and physical therapy at home. I think my insurance paid for some of the sessions and my uncles paid for some as well. My speech therapist's name was Hank. He was a smart guy who knew a lot about the anatomy of speech. He figured out that the back of my tongue wasn't working properly and that was one of the reasons I was having trouble forming certain words. He listened patiently as I tried to repeat words back to him. I had a problem saying words with hard syllables, such as words that started with the letters c, g, and k. To form certain words like "key" and "good," the back of my tongue had to rise to the roof of my mouth. As a result of my accident or of the months I spent unable to speak in the hospital. In any case, part of the muscle in my tongue had become weak. Hank gave me some exercises to strengthen my tongue and to try to improve my speech. I was frustrated by my lack of progress and my inability to speak clearly. I knew how to take apart and fix many things, but I could not fix myself. That was the hardest thing for me to bear. I knew what I wanted, but now I was going to have to depend on others for help.

The physical therapist who came to my home was named Treg. He was okay, except that he got a little mad when I called him Shorty. He helped set up some range-of-motion exercises for my home health aides to help me with to stretch out my limbs. My right leg was a constant source of pain, due to the contracture in it. My dad tried to help by constructing a standing machine out of wood. It was an ingenious design, I have to give him credit, but I hated it. It felt like I was strapped inside some kind of medieval torture device. The way it worked was he and Missy would slide me over from my bed and onto the sheet of plywood that formed the back of the machine. Next, they would strap me down, looping straps over my chest and legs, cinching me down tight to the wood. Next they would slowly tip the whole apparatus upright until it locked into a vertical position. After about fifteen minutes I could not take it anymore, and I wanted down.

The muscles on the right side of my body had become weak due to my accident, causing me to flop over sideways in my wheelchair at times. My right leg would slip off my foot pedal and be drawn up painfully under my seat. Due to the contracture in my leg, this would in turn cause me to lose my balance, leading me to flop over sideways in my chair. At that time I lacked the strength to pull myself upright, so I had to hang there, sideways, until someone helped me up. My dad shoved a piece of foam on the side of my chair as a temporary solution, but I had to figure out a way to fix my leg. Not only to keep it from falling off the footrest, but also for if I was ever going to have a chance to walk again. I sat down with my therapist Treg, and he went over my options with me. I settled on a surgical procedure called a zplasti, which would cut my leg tendons at an angle then sew the ends back together in order to lengthen them, and in turn, straighten my leg. Though very painful, the procedure was a success. I learned that surgery hurts like hell; I don't recommend it. Before I could have the surgery, I was going to have to try to build up my leg muscles up as much as possible. So I began going to physical therapy three times a week during the fall and winter of that year and was slowly getting stronger. I would be going to therapy back at the nursing home where I was once a patient. It was odd at first, being back there. People knew my name, but I didn't know or remember who they were. I would either take the care cab or medivan to and from my appointments. They were two companies who had wheelchair equipped vans, that people could call to be picked up to take to medical appointments.

One of the things they had me do in physical therapy was a StairMaster-type machine. They would wheel my chair up to this machine, and then they would strap my feet to the pedals. I would then have to pump my knees up and down trying to push each pedal down, one at a time. It felt like pedaling a bicycle. At first it was very hard, but after awhile I got the hang of it and it got easier. They let me bring music to therapy, which helped some. It not only helped pass the time, but I also would rather listen to AC/DC or the Rolling Stones while I worked out than the radio, which was always tuned to the country music station. Another thing they did in physical therapy was they would lay me on the mat and then I was supposed to practice rolling over.

I felt like a helpless baby because I could no longer do the simplest of things. Things I once took for granted were now so very hard for me to do. There were a lot of things that I would never be able to do again. Things I took for granted before. For you who are reading this listen up! This is important whatever you think of me or what I have written may not matter. There is one single point that I want to stress to you: Never take things or people for granted. I know you probably think, "Oh nothing will ever happen to me", but everyone knows at least one person who has been hurt or in some kind of accident. Hell, look at Superman: he fell off his horse and broke his neck. What I am trying to say is this: do not waste your life. Life is very short and once it is over you can't get any more of it back. As for the people in your life, do not take them for granted. Everyone is going to need help at some point in his or her lives, and the people in our lives are not always going to be around. So, take nothing for granted, for things can change in the blink of an eye.

My first attempt at walking didn't go so well. By this time, I was able to bear my weight on my feet, for a brief time at least. The problem, once again, was my right leg. When people would pull me up to a standing position, my right foot would barely touch the floor. In physical therapy they wanted to see what I could do. They stood me up and strapped my forearms to a walker. Then, with one person on each side of me to keep me from falling over, I took my first steps since my accident.

I remembered how to walk, that wasn't the problem. The difficulty was getting my body and my legs to cooperate. I took one big step and then another, and soon I was almost sprinting around the physical therapy room. If not for the walker and people on each side to hold me up, I would have landed flat on my face. They walked along side of me trying to keep me up on course. Since my right leg was a bit shorter than the left, it was hard for me to walk in a straight line. Instead, I tended to veer off to the side and walk in a circle. After two laps around the physical therapy room, I was sweaty and exhausted. But I had proved to myself that I could do it.

Around this time I was filling out papers for an application to go to yet another rehab hospital. It was called the Courage Center. It was supposed to be one of the best rehab hospitals in the country, located in Golden Valley Minnesota, a suburb of the Twin Cities. There was a three to six-month waiting list to get in. Also, you had to have an interview before you could even be accepted. My dad helped me out a lot when he could. He bought an old van and he and his friend fashioned a homemade folding ramp out of steel and plywood. Now I didn't have to always be stuck at home. I could now have a little independence to go places. The van was lacking tie-downs to secure my wheelchair to the floor, so my dad improvised by using several heavy-duty bungee cords. For the most part they worked fine, though it did get a little interesting when people would brake suddenly or take turns too sharp.

A month or so after my eighteenth birthday, I started receiving social security. The state had determined that I was now permanently disabled and no longer able to work, so they issued me monthly a check. It was for something like two hundred and thirty dollars—a small windfall for someone who hadn't worked in nearly a year. I remember my little brothers were pretty excited when the first check came in the mail. They thought I was rich, but about half went to my parents for rent. I put some in the bank and some of it went for stupid crap like books, music, some clothes, and a cheap CD/cassette player. I also bought a small, used TV from the pawnshop. I could have made a lot more money in a month if I had been able to work. I was a hard worker. I had my first job when I was seven years old. It was for a small resort down the road from my house; they owned about a dozen old, wooden fishing boats. My job was to bail them out with a bucket and sponge after it would rain. It was hard work. Sometimes it took me most of the day to finish. Growing up my older brothers, my sister, and I all worked. As for me, I did a lot of different things. I mowed lawns, picked rocks, planted and picked strawberries, worked at a grocery store, and I did some roofing and construction. In high school I had two jobs, one as a dishwasher and cook at a small café, the other was doing TV antenna and electronic repair. I would have settled for the worst, shittiest job there was if it meant I could have had my life back.

Now that I had a van, I was able to get out and do things once in awhile, like go to the casino or even go ice fishing. There was a casino on an Indian reservation about twenty miles from my house. My older brother had a job there as a money-changer. Now that I was eighteen I was legal to do a few more things, like vote, buy tobacco, and gamble. It's funny—when I was a kid I couldn't wait to turn fifteen so I could get my driver's permit. Then I couldn't wait to turn sixteen to get my driver's license and to buy my first car. And when you are sixteen years old, you cannot wait until you turn eighteen so you can be an adult. Looking back there is some times when I miss being a kid. I think sometimes being an adult is not always what it's cracked up to be.

The winters in Minnesota were often long and very cold, lasting from the end of October through March or even April. My dad turned an old shed of my grandfather's into a wheelchair-accessible ice-fishing house, complete with windows and a stove. In Minnesota, the lakes freeze over in the wintertime. The ice gets so thick on some lakes that people can drive their cars and trucks on the ice. People would also pull small shacks or ice shanties, as they are sometimes called, onto the frozen lakes in order to fish through the ice. On some of the larger lakes the ice fishing houses are often so plentiful that it would look like a small city had sprung up on the ice. Christmas came and went. I got three different boxes of Trivial Pursuit from my family. That was one game I could play that did not require the use of my vision or my hands. All I needed in order to play was my mind. I found that I was pretty good at remembering obscure facts. I also got a miniature tape recorder that I had asked for, to use with this idea I was working on. My friend Jack bought me something as well: my first book on tape. It was by Robert Ludlum. That first book on tape got me hooked. I enjoyed reading before, but I never had many books of my own, certainly none on audiotape. I now have a small library of my own with a couple hundred titles. I have always enjoyed having things read to me. In school, I was always able to comprehend and process information better if I heard it, than if I read it myself. Since I was now blind and no longer able to read print, this skill would prove to be very useful to me. I was no longer in school, and all of my plans to go to college now seemed to be lost. With no practical means of furthering my education, I began to educate myself. I had a thirst for knowledge. I educated myself the only way I knew how: by listening to books on tape. It may seem like an unorthodox way to learn, and in truth it was, but I was bored a lot of the time and needed something to occupy my mind. I didn't care to watch TV much, as it makes it hard to follow when you can't see what's going on. So I spent a lot of time listening to books on tape. My mom would get the books on tape for me from the library. I would then listen to them one by one until I finished, then I would have her return them and check out several more. The titles always varied and included many different authors and subjects. All in all, I ended up listening to a wide variety of books. One advantage of listening to a book on tape compared to a hard cover or paperback book was that I could now finish a book or novel in a matter of days, where before it might take weeks just to finish one book.

Chapter Twenty

Stormy

The dark heavens have been at war for how long?

Mother Nature does not know.

Blue-white spears of blinding light

Lance the bottoms of the pregnant, swollen black clouds,

Thrusting in the hot, hellish forks.

Bursting open from a million angry wounds,

The misery seeps from the sky

To be lapped up by the greedy, thirsty earth.

The ground shakes and the air trembles

As an avalanche of sound rolls down,

Cascading towards the nervous, quivering ground.

The terrified wind shrieks and howls

Like maddened spirits,

Raking through the treetops.

All is chaos over land and sea:

The heavens are at war,

Leaving the world stormy.

March 9, 1993

This was the day I was to go for my interview at the Courage Center. Not knowing what to expect, I did my best to prepare for it. At this time, I still had a lot of trouble speaking. So my home health aide Missy helped me think of some questions to ask, which she then recorded into my mini tape recorder. They were questions like how long would I have to stay there, and would I be able to go to school? I remember I had five or six questions that she helped record for me. Then, with my little tape recorder tucked securely in my shirt pocket, my parents and I headed south to the city of Golden Valley, where the rehab center was located.

It was a cold and snowy March day; the icy fingers of winter were hanging on as long as possible. After a two-hour drive, I arrived for my interview that morning. Arriving at the Courage center, my dad parked the van in the snow-covered parking lot. Then after unloading my chair from the back, we followed a smooth asphalt path to the front door. These opened in front of us with a silent whoosh. They were automatic doors similar to those at grocery stores. This was just one of the features that made the Courage Center almost totally accessible. Another was the elevators: the buttons on the outside were big, flat disks about eight inches in diameter. So people who could not use their fingers were still able to open the elevator doors. They could bump the button with a fist, elbow, or even a foot. Another thing that helped make the place accessible were the doorknobs to the rooms. Instead of having round knobs that required someone to grasp with one's hand and turn and twist open with one's wrist, they were long levers that could be pushed down to open the door.

My parents were not allowed to go with me to the interview. I was brought to a small office where I was introduced to some people, one of whom was the head nurse of the first floor. His name was Robert. I believe there were more people in the room, but I could not see them, nor can I remember their names. Robert did most of the talking, and I thought he seemed like a nice guy at first. I have to admit that I was very trusting and naïve back then. It is funny how your views of people often change once you are around them for any length of time. During the interview, Robert asked me a bunch of questions like how old I was, and was I on a special diet? He asked how I had heard of the Courage Center. I told him I heard a commercial on TV, and later I was given some information by one of my therapists. Soon it was my turn to ask some questions. I indicated the tape recorder in my shirt pocket. I asked him to take it out and press play. Soon the voice of my home health aide Missy filled the small room. "Question number one: How long would I have to remain here if I was to be accepted at the Courage Center?" He explained that the time was different for everyone, but on average the stays were about ten months to a year. It took a few minutes for me to take that in. To me, a year seemed like a long time. Question number two: "Would I be able to go to school?" The answer was maybe. They did have tutors to help some people with certain tasks. Question number three: "would I be able to get a job and work while I was staying there?" I thought maybe that was a foolish question to ask. I am not sure what job I could possibly have done, but I wanted to do something. I remember his answer was probably not.

When the interview was over, I was reunited with my parents and we were given a tour of the facility. I remember going down the elevator to a hall that led into a large dining room. There were people laughing and joking. The noise of the room sounded a lot like a high school cafeteria. The only difference was that most of the people were in wheelchairs. Our guide called out to one girl who was seated nearby at one of the tables. He inquired how her tennis game was fairing. I thought he was making a cruel joke, for even I could tell she was sitting in a wheelchair. But when she answered "pretty good" I didn't know what to think. How is somebody in a wheelchair able to play tennis? Seeing my confusion, the girl laughed. She then introduced herself; her name was Laura. She also told me some of the rules for wheelchair tennis. It was played basically like regular tennis except for a couple of exceptions: the game was played from a wheelchair, and the ball was allowed to bounce twice before it was hit.

After that, our tour guide took my parents and I to check out some of the rooms. There were quite a few younger people staying there at the time, and the state of their rooms also reflected their ages. We stopped in the open doorway to one room that apparently was shared by a couple of guys. There were a few dirty clothes lying around the room and some pinup posters of girls on the walls. My dad told me about the poster. I think they embarrassed my mom, which I thought was kind of funny. There were two floors of rooms at the center. Both the ground floor and the first floors were set up pretty much the same. At the far end of the hall was a nurse's station and lining the walls down the hallways were rows of rooms. It was sort of set up like a big rectangle, in the middle of which there was a small kitchen area that had some tables and chairs, a refrigerator, and other things like a microwave and a coffeepot. Along one of the walls were two public phones that the residents could use. Seeing these, my mom remarked how some thoughtful person had left menus and coupons for local takeout places next to the phones. What my mom failed to realize, and what I would later learn, was that those menus and coupons were placed there as a public service by the residents.

Ten days later I received a letter in the mail from the Courage Center. It was an acceptance letter along with a list of personal items that I would be allowed to bring. I believe it also gave an approximate date when a bed would be available. The estimated date was about two months away. This gave me time to get things ready and to schedule my leg surgery to fix my contracture.

I went in for surgery March thirty-first, and except for waking up on the operating table with a tube shoved down my throat, the operation went smoothly. I remember I had somehow woken up during the operation. For a few brief moments I was confused and disoriented, not sure where I was. My leg felt good, and for once I felt no spasms but that sensation only lasted for a moment. For that's when great waves of pain began to wash over my body. I began to moan, then to struggle and fight, as I became aware of the hard plastic breathing tube that was placed between my teeth and down my throat. Realizing that I was awake, the anesthesiologist put me under once again. I woke up sometime later in a hospital bed with a cast covering my entire right leg. I felt sick. I wasn't sure if it was from the pain or anesthesia, or if it was a combination of the two. In any case, I felt awful, like I had been drinking all night and I had a bad hangover. Seeing that I was awake, my mom came to the side of my bed. She told me that my home health aide Missy was with her as well. She had stopped by my room to see how I was doing.

I told my mom I was going to be sick. So searching frantically around the room for something for me to throw up in, Missy spotted the trash can in the corner of the room. Snatching it up, she raced back to my bed. That's when things began to happen that were beyond my control. I opened my mouth to speak, and a torrent of hot burning vomit erupted from my insides and shot out my nose and mouth like a fire hose. I hit Missy square in the chest from three or four feet away. It was impressive, in a gross sort of way. She stood there stunned for a few moments with her bucket in her hands. I wasn't sure if she was going to laugh or cry. What do you say to someone that you have just drenched with your puke? Thankfully she had a pretty good sense of humor and was able to laugh about it.

I spent a couple of painful days in the hospital before I was recovered enough to be sent home. They had to create a makeshift sling to keep my leg elevated while I was in my chair for the ride home. I remember cursing out the Medi-van driver when he ran over a pothole or bump in the road. It felt to me as if he ran over every pothole in the road he could find. Arriving home, the driver helped my mom lift me into the bed. I think he was glad to get rid of me. For the next month or so I would be confined to my bed for most of the time. Getting up to eat and use the bathroom was about it. Even this became difficult at times. Just lying in bed all day long I started to become sick and constipated, so my home health aide Missy had to give me medicine to help me go to the bathroom.

My mom had a hard time trying to take care of me by herself. It was hard for me to deal with as well. She was under a lot of stress resulting in us having some arguments. One that I clearly remember, we had said some words I guess and she had had it with me and threatened to put me back in the nursing home. I remember that we were both in tears after that. One of the reasons my mom was so stressed out was because at that time my dad wasn't home. He had gone to Ohio for a couple weeks to help my two uncles with some resort properties that they were developing. My mom really didn't like the Minnesota winters. So my dad agreed to drive down to Ohio to take a look at the project and possibly find a place to resettle his family. They had put the house up for sale the year before with the plans to move to Michigan, but the night before the prospective buyers were supposed to show up to sign the papers, a tornado touched down tearing a swath of destruction through the whole area. The house was untouched but many of the grand old shade trees that grew around the yard were toppled over. I had to give the realtor credit, because the next afternoon he hauled the prospective buyers out in his car. He had to navigate around fallen trees and over downed power lines to get to the house. I think he really wanted to make a sale. Needless to say, it didn't happen for him. The whole yard that my brothers and I had spent mowing and trimming the day before, now looked like a war zone.

The people spent about five minutes tentatively picking their way around the debris-covered lawn, then got back in their car and left. It was about a year after my accident before they were able to sell the house. My parents waited until I went to rehab, then sold the house and moved to Ohio.

I now weighed a little over a hundred pounds. Even so, lying in the same position on my back was starting to take a toll on my body. I developed a pressure sore, or what is also called a bedsore, on my tailbone. A bedsore is where the skin breaks down resulting in an open wound in the skin. Left untreated, they can turn into deep craters, sometimes resulting in hospitalization or, in some cases, death. The skin is the largest organ of the human body and if you have an open wound that is left untreated it can lead to infection. My sore was fairly small, about the size of a quarter, and took a few weeks to completely heal up. My home health aide applied ointment and bandages every day until it was healed. It was literally a pain in the ass. About five weeks after my surgery, I was able to have my cast off and I was given a Velcro leg brace to wear instead. The brace would keep my leg straight while I slept, or when I was up in my chair for awhile. My knee joint was now very stiff and excruciatingly painful to bend. This would continue to give me pain for the next couple of months.

Chapter Twenty-one

Me

You don't know who I am.

You don't care about what I used to do,

Places I have been,

Or things that I have seen.

Who the hell cares?

You don't know me.

Lost in the crowd and overlooked,

Just another face,

One more missing page to your book.

You don't know what I have done,

Or the things that my hands have made.

Who the hell cares anyway?

You don't know me.

I can't be who you want me to be.

I am no longer the man I used to be.

Caught between heaven and hell,

My body and soul scream to be set free.

The things that I want,

I will never have again.

I will never walk again nor see.

Those abilities were stolen from me,

I just want to get away from here,

Find somewhere to disappear,

To run away and just leave.

Nobody here knows me anyway.

June 2, 1993

It had been eighteen months since my accident. I survived my own death, life in a nursing home, and two different hospitals. I was clinically blind, unable to use my hands, or able to walk, also, my speech was very soft and hard to understand. So except for my mind and my sense of hearing, I didn't have much to work with. I was pretty helpless. I was also a very stubborn and a strong-willed person who didn't give up very easily. I had one dream or goal at that time, which was to live as independently as possible. I didn't know yet how I was going to accomplish such a thing, or if it would be possible, but I was going to try. So on a warm day in June, I found myself back at the Courage Center. Their facility and rehab program was supposed to teach people with disabilities the skills that would allow them to become and to live independently. Those are things I was going to have to learn. On June 2, 1993, I became a patient at the Courage Center. I would remain there for exactly one year and two days.

Arriving at the Courage Center the second time was a lot different. For one thing, I was able to observe a lot more of my surroundings. Now that the snow was gone, the grounds outside were surprisingly well-landscaped. There were paths through the trees along with flower beds. There was also a small creek that wound its way through the property; it was spanned by two small bridges; one of wood, and the other of concrete and stone.

When I got there, my parents and I had to fill out some more papers, and the staff also explained some of the rules to us. One of the rules was while I was staying there they would take away my social security payments. This was to help pay for my care, I guess. Instead I was given an allowance of fifty-six dollars a month. This was for personal items such as laundry soap, shampoo, and stuff like that. I would soon become adapt at managing and saving the small amount of money that I was allowed each month. I used a lot of it to relieve the monotony and boredom of the place. Some of the residents pissed away their whole allowance on the vending machines each month. I preferred to save my money for concert tickets, music CDs, and the occasional bottle of whiskey.

As for most of the other rules, I would have to figure them out for myself. After filling out the papers I was shown to my room, which was on the first floor at the end of the hall. It had two hospital beds, two small dressers, and two nightstands. There was a bathroom with a roll-in shower, and there was also a walk-in closet across from the bathroom. There was a sliding door that led to a small balcony.

As for my things, I was only allowed to bring so much. They didn't allow you to bring large TVs or stereo systems. You also had to have your name on all of your things, including all of your clothing: underwear, socks, and even shoes. All I brought was my CD player, a case of music tapes, some clothes, a pair of sneakers, and some toiletry items like an electric razor and a toothbrush. As my mom helped me put my things away, I met the first of four roommates I would have during my stay at the Courage Center. He rolled through the doorway pushing himself in his wheelchair. His name was Danny and he seemed like an okay guy. I believe he was from Wisconsin. I didn't have a chance to get to know him very well, because he left after the first week I was there.

After my parents left, I was on my own. It took some getting used to and I had a lot to think about. I stayed pretty much to myself those first few days. I remember being yelled at my first night there. I had to use the toilet, and the aide placed a towel over my lap for privacy, I had an accident and peed on the towel a little bit. When she came back I told her what had happened. I was embarrassed. I remember she got very angry and told me that's not how things were done here! She didn't take the time to listen to me or anything I had to say. Later, she walked in and threw a sheet of laminated paper down on my lap and then walked out without a word. I didn't know what it was, or what it was for, or what it said. I could not see it. I wanted to tell her to shove it up her ass but I didn't. Later, I found out that the paper was an alphabet board. It had the letters of the alphabet printed on it. I was supposed to point to the letters and spell out what I needed. For one thing I could not see the damn thing to read it in the first place, nor could I use my hands to point at the letters.

I did not yet know what kind of place I was in, and I didn't want to make any enemies if I could help it. For in truth, I was all alone and a little scared. The aides at the Courage Center were called RA's, which stood for resident assistant. I would soon learn which ones were good and could be counted on, and which ones were lazy, or mean, or fell asleep on the job. For the most part they were pretty nice, and I got to know a lot of them fairly well during my stay there. The Courage Center was a cross between a college dorm, hospital, insane asylum, and prison, all wrapped up together under one roof. But for all of us who had to live there, I think my friend Scott summed it up best when he declared he was stuck on the Island of Misfit Toys. He was referring to the cartoon *Rudolf the Red-Nosed Reindeer*, when Rudolph and his pals took a wrong turn and landed on the Island of Misfit Toys. It was true for all of us who lived at the Courage Center, for we were all broken or disfigured in some way or another. We were all misfits now.

The first couple weeks I spent there were very frustrating and very boring. I had to wait for my doctor's orders for treatment to be approved before I could start any of my therapies. After about three days spent alone in my room with nothing to do, I asked one of the RAs to push me out to the kitchen area. Most of the residents owned power wheelchairs, or could walk or could get around by themselves. But I had to be pushed everywhere I went, which was a big pain. The kitchen was a common area where many of the residents would hang out in the evening or between therapy sessions or classes. It was a place where residents could smoke, drink coffee, listen to the radio, or just hang out and talk. I had the RA put my tape case and a couple of my CDs on my lap before pushing me out to the kitchen. There was a small stereo out there. I remember thinking that "at least this way I wouldn't have to listen by myself." Thinking back, I would have been better off if I had stayed in my room. The RA pushed me up to the table where some people where sitting, then was called away to help someone else.

One girl asked my name and I was quickly introduced around the table. I found out her name was Susan. Apparently, she had been a bit wild back in the day and had been in a motorcycle accident, which had damaged her spine. I found out all of this after the first five minutes of sitting down. She was a bit loud and obnoxious at times, one of those people who thinks they know everything and will cut you down as soon as you leave the room. But of course I didn't know that at the time, being trusting and naïve of people and of the real world. I would soon learn for myself that people were often not what they seemed to be. During her stay, she would annoy so many of the other residents that they organized a betting pool on what day and hour she would leave. One dollar bought a five-minute block of time. The pool was up to almost fifty bucks by the time she left. I just missed it by ten minutes.

Another resident at the table was a kid named David. He rolled up to the table where I was sitting. I try never to judge people and treat them how I would like to be treated, but this guy David was the most vile, lazy, disgusting person I had ever met. I think he had a disease called spinabifida and he used a wheelchair to get around, but could walk with crutches if he wanted to. He was able to do everything for himself if he chose to. He could feed himself, dress himself, transfer himself; he was also able to take himself to the bathroom and shower by himself, which I think he rarely did. Instead, he would sit in his own shit and piss all day long, not because he was mentally deficient and didn't know any better, he was just lazy, so he went in his pants. His room was at the end of the hall across from the kitchen, and it could be smelled from down the hall if the door was open. It made me mad. Here I was, trying so hard to improve my situation and could hardly do anything for myself, and he could do so much for himself and had twenty-one or twenty-two years to improve his situation, but was too lazy to try.

Not all of the residents who lived there were bad. In fact, most of them were pretty cool, but I tried to avoid a few of them when I could. I ended up meeting a lot of interesting people who had all different types of disabilities. Most of us were just trying to get on with our lives; which granted, was harder for some than others. There were people there who had been in car accidents, and had received bad head injuries. There were people who had broken their necks in all kinds of ways; from car wrecks, to falling off a ladder, to going skinny-dipping and diving into the river drunk, to riding a toboggan down a snowy hill. Even just wrestling around, one kid hit the back of his neck on a rock and broke it. There were people who had suffered strokes, people with multiple sclerosis, muscular dystrophy, and cerebral palsy as well. It was a very different place to live.

I had a room to myself for the first couple of months, which was okay by me. Since my roommate Danny left, I was alone. The only problem was that I couldn't really call for help. The RA would check in on me from time to time, or hang out with me on the balcony (I spent as much time as possible outside). But the nights were the worst for me. I had a narrow hard-ass hospital bed, which I fell out of two times during my stay. I hated that bed. My feet and ankles would get caught in the bed rails, and I would have to yell for help until someone came to untangle me. After that, they started to wrap blankets around the bed rails. I didn't get much sleep while I was there.

After about two weeks I began my therapies. The first class I went to was called music therapy. I personally thought it was pretty stupid. A guy named Mark came and got me from my room. At first, I thought he was one of the RAs, but I soon found out he was one of the residents. He could walk and talk—he seemed perfectly normal to me. I later found out that he was recovering from a surgery to remove a tumor from his brain. He had a slight limp when he had to walk long distances, but other than that, you could not tell anything was wrong with him. He told me that he was from Atkin, Minnesota. I was excited because

Atkin was only fifteen miles from my hometown of Garrison. He was several years older than me and told me that he went to school with my cousin Liz. We soon became fast friends. He was a nice guy. He was one of the people who kind of looked out for me, for example, he often volunteered to push my chair when we had outings. We also ate lunch together sometimes.

The music therapy class was at the far end of the hall in an all-purpose meeting room called the Fireside Lounge. The room contained a couple of long tables, along with a mess of chairs. There was also a small fireplace along the far wall that may or may not have worked at one time. Around the table sat some of the other residents. I soon found out that what we all had in common was that we all had head injuries. When a person receives a head injury, their emotions and personality can often change. I was introduced around the room to some of the other residents. There was only one other person in the room, besides me, who was in a wheelchair; her name was Robin. She had been on her way home from a softball game when she was involved in a car accident. She broke her neck and also sustained a head injury as a result of the accident. She could not speak; instead she used a computerized communication device. I'm not sure how it exactly worked, but I believed she had a switch that she was able to squeeze with her hand. I remember she would tease people, and in spite of all that had happened to her she still had a great sense of humor. She was an amazing girl.

There was another guy named Mark, who I believe had suffered a stroke. His speech was slurred at times, but other than that I could not tell there was anything wrong with him. He was a funny guy, always cracking jokes to make people laugh. There was a guy named Curt who wrecked his car drinking and driving; he was a pretty nice guy as well. He said that before his accident he was keeping Budweiser in business. He now had to wear an eye patch to keep from having double vision and to help him keep his balance when he walked. I also think it gave him incentive to quit drinking.

There was a girl named Jenny who was also in a car accident. She was quiet and soft-spoken and mostly kept to herself. She was a nice person and always kind to me. There was also a guy named C.J. I didn't like him; he was very spooky. He would be nice one minute, and in an instant his attitude could change and he would be mean as a snake. He was unpredictable. I did my best to stay away from him. There was Molly. She was a Chippewa Indian from Hayward, Wisconsin. Lastly, there was an older guy named Bernie. I am not sure what had happened to him. Someone told me that he was once a respiratory technician. I don't know if that was true or not, but what whatever knowledge he once had was pretty much gone. He had to be reminded of things like when to eat and even his own name. I felt sorry for him. What I remember most about Bernie was the tomato. He had grown a tomato plant out on his balcony and it had produced a tomato. He would carry it around with him wherever he went and when people would ask him about it his face would light up as he told them how he grew it.

There really wasn't much that was musical about music therapy, but if they called it group therapy no one would want to go. I personally thought it was dumb; not the residents, but the therapist who were in charge. After awhile I quit going.

Meal times at the Courage Center were often bad. The food made Sister Kenny's hospital food seem like gourmet cuisine. I now knew the reasons for all of the menus and coupons that were posted by the phones. There was a hierarchy of sorts when it came to getting meals. At the top of the list were those who were ambulatory or could walk, next were those who could move themselves along in their wheelchairs. Lastly at the bottom of the list were those who needed help eating and who had to be fed; I fell into this category. They called us "feeders." I hated that word. I tried different methods of trying to feed myself while I was at the Courage Center. In occupational therapy, they tried strapping a fork to my wrist. I had difficulty trying to get the food to my mouth. The contracture in my wrist prevented me from turning it in order to scoop or pick food up on the fork, so they made a goofy bent fork for me to try. This worked somewhat. I was able to bring the fork to my mouth but someone first had to stab the food on the fork for me, which limited the foods I was able to eat with my crazy fork. I found that the only foods that worked really well were grapes and chicken nuggets, and I am allergic to chicken. They also had me test out a device called a feeding machine which was actually pretty cool. It was a plate that would rotate when you hit a toggle switch, and then another switch would activate a mechanical spoon. It was like something out of *Back to the Future*. With this machine I was able to feed myself. They made a video of me using it and everything. But the machine turned out to be just a prototype, so I wasn't able to get one. Also, my insurance would not cover it. They said that feeding myself was not deemed to be a medical necessity.

I did not gain much weight while living there. They would weigh us about once a month, and I remained at 114 pounds. They ordered double portions for me, along with these nasty milk shakes for snacks. I ate a lot of peanut butter and jelly along with lots of takeout pizza. In the mornings for breakfast one of the residents, I believe her name was Alice, used to sneak me donuts from the conference room. She was an older lady. I am not sure what had happened to her that she ended up there, but she was very nice. She also sort of looked out for me. I was fortunate to have friends and people watch out for me while I was there; otherwise, I doubt I could have made it by myself. Living there gave me a chance to learn a lot about people. I was able to relate to a lot of the residents, for I knew how it felt to live with a disease, having lived with asthma most of my life.

Though I apparently no longer suffered from asthma, I still had a lot of problems to contend with. Some of the residents would ask me what level I was, referring to what vertebrae I had broken in my neck. At first I didn't know what they were talking about, but I eventually realized that to them I seemed paralyzed. Though I may have had symptoms of paralysis, I was able to feel everything and also to move my arms and legs. I also had a lot of spasticity in my muscles and some difficulty with my speech. These were symptoms of cerebral palsy; though I didn't have it some people assumed I did. And even though I was considered legally blind I was still able to see a little bit enough to make a few things out. I was able to memorize my surroundings and fake the rest. So if people didn't know I was blind, they would assume I could see. I don't know why I chose not to reveal that I was blind. I wanted to appear as independent and normal as possible, even though I knew I wasn't. I didn't want to be treated differently. Also, sometimes when people would find out I could not see some of them would act weird around me, or talk real loud like I was deaf and could not hear. That would piss me off; I hated that. Even though I didn't agree, I was labeled a quadriplegic or a quad. I hated that word.

After a time, my days began to fall into some semblance of a routine. In the morning one of the RA's would get me up and give me a shower. Then, depending on the time, one of them would push me down to the cafeteria or to the kitchen for breakfast, then I would proceed to my different classes or therapies until late afternoon. The evenings the residents and I had to ourselves to do whatever, sit outside, play cards, watch TV, and listen to music or smoke. It was very boring at times. As for me, I tried to spend as much time outside as possible. I preferred to be outside where I could listen to the wind and water, the birds singing in the treetops, and where I could feel the warm sun on my face. I think for me that was the best therapy: to get away from people for awhile and immerse myself in the sights, sounds, and smells of nature. I think it helped me a lot to cope with things.

In the mornings I would often sit at a table in the kitchen with one or two other residents before I had to leave for my therapies. One of which was a guy named Scott, and he was a nice guy. He had worked for a fire department before he had an accident that resulted in him breaking his neck. Apparently he was putting a new roof on a pole barn or shed. He was at the top of a ladder pounding nails into one of the eaves. As he swung the hammer down he missed the eave and his hammer blow ended up in empty space. This in turn caused him to lose his balance plummeting off the ladder landing head first into the ground. Anyway, like I said he was a nice guy. He used to read the newspaper to me and also tell me which of the RA's were good-looking, giving me details on certain parts of their anatomies.

Chapter Twenty-two

Time

I got nothing to do and all day to do it.

I've got nowhere to go and all day to get there.

I've got nothing to say but who the hell cares?

All I have is time, time to sit, time to think.

Time to plan the perfect crime.

Time floats by like a cloud in the sky.

It trickles through the hourglass so slowly,

One grain of sand at a time.

It ticks away at the wall clock as I watch the minutes pass by.

There is not much to do here.

I am bored out of my gourd, most of the time

I try to keep busy, just to pass the time.

Time, Time, Time.

I got way too much time.

Residents continued to be discharged and new ones would take their place. With a waiting-list to get in, the beds were seldom empty. The new residents would arrive looking a bit overwhelmed and nervous at first, but soon they would make new friends and start to fit in. Some of the residents who had been there awhile and were veterans would teach the new ones little things to help them get along, like how to light a cigarette when your hands don't work so well because you have a broken neck and are paralyzed. About this time I got a new roommate. His name was Don. He was from Fergus Falls, Minnesota. He was a tough kid who used to play football. I believe he rolled his truck while drinking and driving, receiving a head injury in the process. We got along pretty well; he didn't say much and he never did anything to me. The only problem I had was when he would come into the room and get ready for bed about two in the morning. He would put his Van Halen tape in his clock radio and turn the volume up full blast. I would yell at him to turn it down. He would apologize and turn it down a little bit. He only owned the one tape, so after about three nights of Van Halen I gave up. When the tape was over he would go to sleep— I guess it was a nighttime ritual for him. I got pretty sick of Van Halen after awhile, and like I said before, I didn't get much sleep while I was there.

Due to the accident, or maybe that's just how he was, in any case Don had some problems behaving. He would get grabby with many of the female RA's. He also got into some fights with some of the other residents. He was very strong, so most people stayed clear of him. He had some unusual habits as well, one of which was eating chewing tobacco. He would buy a sack of Red Man then proceed to eat the whole bag. I had never seen anyone eat chewing tobacco before. As far I knew he never got sick. Another one of his habits was to roam the halls in his wheelchair late at night, with no pants on. But in spite of all that he was an okay guy. He was harmless unless someone made fun of him or did something to make him mad. There was one incident were Don sent one of the janitors to the hospital. I don't know what had happened; I believe Don was helping him move some chairs in the kitchen. I don't now if they were just horsing around or what, but I think Don may not have known his own strength. In any case a chair ended up being swung, catching the janitor in the back, sending him to the floor and to the hospital. When the head nurse, Robert, found out, he went to the kitchen to confront Don. He tried to pick a fight with Don by taunting him, goading Don to take a swing at him. Robert thought he was hot shit because he was in the National Guard. Yet, there he was, trying to pick a fight with one of the residents so he could have an excuse to get rid of him. But Don just rolled past him in his chair, ignoring him. I lost all respect for Robert after that. Also after that, Don had to move to a single room in order to have less contact with the other residents and the staff, I guess.

One of the things that I was required to do while at the Courage Center was to meet with a psychologist once a week. Her name was Lea. She was a nice girl but she didn't help me much. I was an angry young man at the time. My parents had just sold their house, so I no longer had a home to return to. Plus, I had no idea what kinds of drugs the doctors pumped into me at the nursing home after my accident. I found out later they had me on eleven different medications at the time. I didn't know what kind of side-effects they may have had, or if they were to blame for my condition. I felt helpless and angry. There was no one to blame; I was mad at the world. After awhile, I realized being angry at everything was useless. It wasn't going to help me get on with my life. In the end, it was the residents who helped me, not the psychologist. I remember sitting outside in the sun with one of the ground-floor residents, Troy, who had broken his neck. After sizing me up, he turned to me and in a cocky voice, he asked me what I used to do? I was a little startled and unsure about how to reply. Then after a few moments I answered him telling him only one word: everything. Then after a minute of silence, he answered me in a quiet voice. He said "me too."

There was a girl named Chris on my floor, who had broken her neck in a diving accident. She was an honest and open person and also a friend. Talking with her helped a lot; it was nice to know that I was not alone when it came to feelings of depression, helplessness, and anger.

We laughed together over the absurdity of life, and cried together over the absurdity of life as well. She had a strong spirit, and I admired her a lot, she was a very cool person. There were a lot of cool people I got to know during my stay there. There was a kid name John. They called him Hell Boy. He had cerebral palsy and used a power wheelchair to get around. He was not able to speak. He used a computerized communication device to speak for him, and he didn't take shit from anyone. If someone tried, he would instantly type back a witty, sarcastic remark of his own. You could always hear him coming, for two reasons. The first reason: John flew everywhere he went in his power chair. He always had it turned up as fast as it could go. The second reason: he was rarely without his Walkman and his heavy metal music, like Metallica and Megadeth, which he always listened to at full-blast. The day before he left the Courage Center for his own apartment, we both got drunk on Jack Daniels in my room. It was a good way to say good-bye.

There was a guy named Donald L. He had cerebral palsy as well. He was an interesting fellow; he had a lot of stories. He was from Iowa, and when he was a kid he spent close to eleven years in the state hospital. I don't know if people thought he was mentally retarded because he could not speak well at the time. In any case, he turned out to be a very intelligent man, and he eventually went to college to study genetics and later began raising German Shepherds and wolf-hybrids. He had a photo album that contained many of his animals that he raised over the years. We became good friends. He had a lot of crazy stories about his life and things that he had done, along with some horror stories of his time in the state hospital.

Donald L was in his forties when I first met him and I learned the crazy story of how he ended up at the Courage Center. Donald also used a power wheelchair to get around and wore braces on his legs to keep them straight. He called them his exoskeleton. The story he told me that led to his arrival at the Courage Center, I thought to be so weird as to be not true. Apparently somehow he had managed to accidentally break or fracture his own neck. He had been sleeping on the couch and one of his friends thought it would be a funny practical joke to wake him by pulling him, feet-first, off the couch. His head struck the hardwood floor in the process. For the next few days he complained of a stiff neck he told me, but didn't think anything of it. He said he had difficulty turning his head to the side because it seemed to be cocked at a funny angle. He told me that he was trying to reach for a book on a shelf but was becoming frustrated because he was unable to turn his head to see where he was reaching. Getting frustrated and a bit angry he decided to fix the problem himself. So reaching up he proceeded to twist or yank his neck back into place. He told me later that it felt like a bomb had went off inside his head. He also said he saw stars for hours afterwards. Eventually he went to the hospital, where the neurosurgeons operated to repair the damage. They told him he was very lucky and was expected to make a full recovery over time.

A few days after Don B. moved out, I got a new roommate named Tommy. He and his wife, Brenda, had been involved in a car accident together. Before coming to the Courage Center, they had been at the Sister Kenny rehab hospital. They both had suffered injuries from the accident. She had a problem moving one of her legs; I am not sure what other disabilities she may have had. As for her husband Tommy, he was not as lucky. He had suffered a severe brain injury as a result of the crash and was no longer able to speak. He would grunt or shake the bed rails if he was mad or wanted attention. He was a good roommate at first, not causing any problems. He was not able to control his bladder, so he had to wear a catheter, this he would pull off during the night not aware of what he was doing or in order to touch himself. Anyway, this would result in him wetting the bed night after night. After awhile, the stench was so awful that I didn't want to be in my own room. I even bought some cans of air fresheners to help with the smell, but the RA's ended up using them instead. I began to spend the least amount of time in my room as possible and stayed up most nights sitting in the kitchen, with the other night owls, in an attempt to avoid my smelly room as much as possible. I would spend just enough time to catch a couple hours of sleep and take a shower. After a couple of weeks, the lack of sleep started to catch up with me. I passed out a couple of times, and fell out of my chair in the process. I even fell asleep on one of the mats in physical therapy, which was sort of embarrassing.

I didn't know what to do. I could not handle the smell, and I could not continue to go without sleep. Even after the RA's changed Tommy's mattress, things did not improve. The mattress had started to mold and rot from the nightly soaking of fluids. I asked if I could change rooms, and the nurses told me no. So I waited, and when I found out my friend Scott was being discharged, I asked his roommate if I could move in and take his place. He said yes and this time the nurses agreed to let me change rooms. After that things got better. My new roommate was a guy named Russ. He was a pretty cool guy; he was a couple of years older than me, and also in a wheelchair. He told me that he was driving home from a house party where he had been drinking when his car went off the road, crashing into a telephone pole or a tree. That's how he broke his neck.

There was a girl, named Deanne, who lived on my floor. She told me she had MS, multiple sclerosis. She helped me out a lot with things, like reading my mail and helping me eat if I ordered pizza. She was pretty cool as well and we hung out a lot. We became friends and started dating, if you could call it dating. I had dated a couple girls in high school, but I had not been with anyone since my accident. I don't know, I thought nobody would want to be with someone who was in a wheelchair; I guess I was wrong. It turns out I was wrong about many things. Anyway, she began staying with me nights when my roommate Russ would go home on weekends. I got some crap from some of the RA's because they all knew what was going on, but for the most part they left us alone; we were both adults.

Chapter Twenty-three

The Invisible Man

In this day and age, people still don't know, nor can they

Understand, how it feels to be an invisible man.

I'm lost in a sea of people, as the people pass by without a care.

For nobody wants to stop and help the man in the wheelchair.

It used to bother me, being ignored like that.

I would get so angry and so mad.

You would be surprised how rude some people can be;

It's actually pretty sad.

It's not easy being an invisible man.

People don't even give you the time of day, or

Take the time to listen to what it is you have to say.

It's not easy being an invisible man.

I try to work hard and do the best I can,

But it's not easy being an invisible man.

I believe everything happens for a reason;

Perhaps it's just part of Gods plan

For me to be an invisible man.

The physical therapy department was like the nerve center of the Courage Center—it was a very busy place. It was where people attempted to relearn the skills that they had lost due to illness or injury. In addition to the residents who lived there, they also had an outpatient treatment program that treated people of all ages, from as young as two years old to senior citizens. As you entered to the right there were some curtained treatment rooms, and further down the hall to the left were offices. In the middle of the floor was a set of horizontal bars about four feet high. They were spaced about three feet apart, so people could hold on to them to practice walking. There were two raised mats; one on each end of the room. On the far wall there stood a standing table and on the opposite wall there were some free weights and an exercise machine that used some kind of pulley system.

The physical therapy department was often a noisy and painful place, but I think the best rehab tool they had was the radio that they had set up there. It was always tuned to KQRS, the classic rock station. As far as I know, it was never turned off. Music was important to me; it was one thing I was able to do by myself. It helped distract me from the pain in my body and also helped me to focus on my workouts.

At the Courage Center most of it was about setting goals. Most of it was common sense and a waste of time I thought, but some people there needed the regimen of a routine. I tried to set my own goals, like saving my money for things I wanted, such as concert tickets or the occasional bottle of whiskey. Later the only goal I had was to get out of the Courage Center, but in order to do so I was going to have to figure some things out. I needed to be patient and wait.

In physical therapy, I told them I was going to walk. At first the physical therapist was skeptical I think. Her name was Amy. She was a small, tough woman who could pick people up and toss them around with ease. I wasn't stupid; I knew that I would have to first build up the muscles in my legs—no easy task for someone who had been sitting on his butt for over a year. By this time I had discarded my leg brace; it would pinch my skin and pull the hair on my leg, so I said the hell with it and threw it away. I told Amy that I wanted first to try standing up. This she did by first cinching a belt tightly around my waist, then after slipping her fingers under it she braced my feet and hoisted me up into a standing position. I was nearly a foot taller than she was and towered over her, but she did her best to hold me upright. The muscles in my back and right side were weak from lack of use, so I tended to flop over a bit from one side or another but she held me steady. After about fifteen minutes of this, she sat me back in my chair. We had both gotten a workout.

The therapist did exercises on the mat with me to help stretch out my legs and also to build up my back and trunk muscles. I also began doing knee bends to help strengthen my legs. I had to try to fix myself. I didn't have a manual or blueprint to follow, and I had to make most of it up myself. So I thought of trying to do some knee bends. Amy would stand me up and hold on to the belt while I tried. At first they were very hard to do; I was only able to do a few before I had to sit down, sweaty and exhausted. But after a few weeks, it became easier. I also stood up in the standing table, which is a machine that holds you in the upright position with straps, to build up some stamina. This did not hurt as bad, now that I had had my surgery. Soon I was ready to attempt walking with a walker. Amy and another therapist stood me up in the hall and strapped my arms to a walker. Then I attempted to take my first steps since my surgery. Unfortunately, it didn't go too well. The problem was that my legs were so tight that with each step my legs would try to cross and I would end up tripping myself. Not how I had planned at all. It was not only frustrating, but disappointing as well. After all of the pain and hard work that I had gone through, I was now so close but my body would not cooperate. Finally, one of the therapists suggested using a brace on my foot to keep it from turning in. It was called an AFO and with this on my left foot I was able to do a lot better.

It took a little practice to find my gait, and I still needed two people to help, but damn it I was walking. It soon became a daily thing and I was allowed to keep the walker and foot brace in my room. Every day after lunch, two of the RA's would help me practice walking. After awhile, I was sprinting down the halls in my walker and the RA's had to walk fast to keep up. I still sometimes veered to the right and occasionally tripped myself. Sadly, I knew that I would never be able to walk on my own. I did not have the balance, but it sure felt good to be up on my feet.

I needed a way to get around; having to depend on people to push me everywhere sucked. I could not use my hands or feet to move my chair. Apparently, I was not the only person who could not move their hands and feet. I soon learned that there were all kinds of different types of controls and switches for power wheelchairs. Anything from a chin switch, to a head control; there was even something for people who could not move at all. It was called a siff and puff. It was basically a straw that one blew and sucked air through. It was similar to Morse code, in a way. A certain number of puffs on the straw would move the chair forward, left or right, and even reverse. It took a lot of breath control to use a siff and puff. I tried it once and I was not able to master it.

Most of the residents had their own power wheelchairs already. I wanted the freedom and independence that my own power wheelchair would offer me. In physical therapy, I was able to try out a power wheelchair with a head control. It was a bit tricky to operate at first, but I soon got the hang of it. The therapist sent in an evaluation and doctor's order for me to get my own power wheelchair, but my insurance company denied my claim.

I was pretty upset about being denied. I didn't want to be stuck in a pushchair for the rest of my life, unable to go anywhere by myself, and depending on other people to push me everywhere. I didn't think I could have handled that. So Amy resubmitted her evaluation and doctors orders, and once again I was denied. This time the insurance company that was called MA, which stood for Medical Assistance, sent me a letter. The letter basically stated that I was being denied a power chair because I had poor vision and I would not be able to operate a power chair safely. I was pissed off at the insurance company. They didn't know what I could and could not do; they had never even met me. Yes, I had poor vision, but I could see enough to make things out and find my way around. I didn't know what to do. I didn't think I had any options, but Amy told me that I still had one option. I could request a hearing with the insurance company, so that's what I did.

I learned about my rights as a patient and the right to subpoena witnesses to speak on my behalf. I was given one day to practice with the power chair, and the next day Amy followed me around with a video camera and recorded me while using the power chair. I now had video evidence proving that I was able to operate a power chair safely. On the day of my hearing, I was shown into a small conference room that was adjacent to the cafeteria. In the room, sitting around the table were representatives from the insurance company, one of the nurses, and one of the physical therapists that I had subpoenaed. In the room there also stood a TV and a VCR on a wheeled stand. After dimming the lights, I made those insurance people watch a video of me driving a power wheelchair. These were the same people who denied me, telling me it wasn't possible for me to drive and that I would be unsafe. When the video was over, the insurance people hemmed and hawed a bit, because they had nothing to say. There was nothing they could say. The next time the papers were submitted they were approved and about six or seven months later I received my first power wheelchair.

For those of you who are reading this and know of someone who tried or is trying to get a piece of medical equipment such as a power wheelchair or anything else, the best advice I can offer you is to not give up. If you are denied, you have the right to appeal, and if you cannot speak, you also have the right to have someone speak on your behalf. The whole process may seem overwhelming and confusing; it was for me the first time I tried to figure it out. But you should not give up. You need to be persistent. The red tape can last for months and sometimes years.

I am going to tell you how to begin the process, in hopes that it may help people and their families. The first thing you need is a prescription from a doctor for the piece of equipment that you need, say it's a power chair for instance. Next, depending where you are at, you will need an evaluation from a physical therapist. You will need a doctor's order for this as well. If it is a wheelchair you are trying to get, the therapist will first have to determine and document if there is a need. Explain to the therapist any medical problems you're having and how you will benefit from the piece of equipment. The more documentation that you can present may work in your favor. Next, the therapist will have to measure you for the piece of equipment you need. This is especially important if it is for a wheelchair; it is important that it fits well. If you need to, you can have them measure you twice to get the most precise measurement. You should also have someone from the medical supply company that you plan to use come out and measure you as well. The reason it is so important that your equipment fit, is because that depending on the state that you live in and your insurance company, you may have to wait anywhere from three to five years before you can be eligible for a new wheelchair; that's a long time to be uncomfortable. Finding a medical supply company in your area may be a problem. Not all of them carry equipment such as wheelchairs. If you live in a small town you can check in the phone book or ask a therapist or social worker to send you a list of vendors. Once the physical therapist has completed the evaluation and other paperwork they will send the prescription and evaluation to the vendor, who will then submit it to the insurance company for approval. This will take anywhere from three to six weeks—maybe more. If you are denied for any reason, you may have to do it all over again, so don't give up.

At the Courage Center I had more therapies than just physical therapy. I had occupational therapy, speech therapy, recreational therapy, and art therapy as well. Art therapy was kind of a joke, but it gave me something to do. There was an RA named Dalton. He had seen some of my woodcarvings I had done and that I had set up in my room. We started talking and I found out he was an artist, a painter and he offered to teach me how to paint. The next day he brought some tubes of watercolor paint, a plastic pallet with depressions for the different colors of paint, along with a tablet of watercolor paper. He explained the different materials to me and how they were used. Next, he fitted a paintbrush in my hand and tried to guide my arm over the paper, which didn't work so well. For one thing, I had to put newspapers down so as not to paint all over the table and myself. Also, my hand was not able to hold on to the paintbrush very well. I thought about holding the paintbrush in my teeth, for I had read of people painting that way. This turned out to be difficult as well because the paintbrush was very hard and smooth, making it difficult to hold in my teeth, it kept slipping out. That night, I went to bed thinking about the problem, and in the morning I had a solution. I went to the store and purchased a set of mouth guards, the kind football and hockey players use. I took them back to the Courage Center and had Dalton heat them up in a bowl of water in the microwave. When they got hot enough, I put them in my mouth to form around my teeth. Then, using half a tongue depressor and some tape, Dalton attached the paintbrush to my mouth guard. I had just invented a mouth-stick paintbrush. Later I had found out the idea had already been invented, and I had a much nicer one built in the Courage Center workshop.

After awhile people heard about my painting and I started meeting with a woman in art therapy about once a week. She knew about water coloring and she taught me some different techniques, like soaking the paper in water first so the paint will bleed more, also how to crumple and crease the paper all over first, before soaking, for a different effect. She even taught me how you could sprinkle salt over the paint, and then after it had dried remove the salt with a rubber eraser. This would give a soft, fuzzy look to the painting.

In recreational therapy we basically planned and went on outings to places like Target, the zoo, the Mall of America (which I thought was obscenely huge), and even places like the state fair. For the outings, most of the time we would take the Metro bus, which was equipped with wheelchair lifts. They also had two vans at the Courage Center that people could sign out, and I also had my van there as well. My parents had left it behind when they moved. So I wasn't always stuck at the Courage Center.

In occupational therapy they didn't do much because I could not use my hands. They did fashion a water bottle and straw that could attach to my chair. They also ordered a signature stamp for me, which made things much more convenient. Before that, someone had to stick a pen between my fingers and hold up whatever I had to sign, so I could try to make an X.

My speech therapist was named Claudia. I didn't care for her. She did not listen very well, and I felt like she thought I was stupid. She gave me exercises to do, but as far as my speech she did not listen. I could not say certain words, so I would substitute a different word with the same meaning that I could say. When I tried to explain this to her she did not listen. She tried to have me use a computerized communication device, but I was not able to use my hands. So she had them rig up a big button behind the head of my wheelchair. The device was very awkward and painstakingly slow to use. How it worked was, it would scroll through the alphabet one letter at a time, and I was to hit the button when I heard the letter that I wanted. Then I was to keep adding letters until I had a word. If I happened to miss a letter and if I hit the button at the wrong time, I would have to wait until the whole alphabet scrolled through. I tried, but it was very hard to time the button just right and I could not get it to work. The whole process was extremely slow and frustrating. When I told her that I didn't like the machine and that I didn't want to use it, the speech therapist got angry. Years later, I would invent and have built a simple, effective communication device of my own design, based on Morse code. I would also use it to write while taking some college classes. Eventually, I would use this device to write the book you are now reading. But before I was to attempt writing anything I was going to first have to learn how to spell. I admit I am not one of the world's best spellers. I know a lot of words, but that doesn't mean I know how to spell all of them.

At the Courage Center I tried to keep busy because a lot of the time things were boring and I had nothing to do. I wanted to read, but my vision was too poor to read even jumbo print. I thought about learning Braille but dismissed the idea because of my hands. Then I remembered reading a story somewhere about a blind man who had read the entire bible in Braille, using the tip of his tongue. I thought that was pretty cool, but at the same time I didn't want to be the next guy in line to read that book. Anyway, it gave me an idea to try, so I got in touch with someone from the Minnesota Institute for the Blind. They sent a guy to meet with me. His name was Bob and he was blind as well. I told him about my idea of reading in Braille with my tongue, and he agreed to try to teach me. So, on his next visit he brought with him several sheets of laminated paper that had Braille printed on them. Then after wiping the sheets of plastic paper with an alcohol pad to kill any germs, he arranged the papers out on a small table in my room. Now it was my turn to try out my idea. As I leaned over the table, I began exploring the paper with the tip of my tongue. I felt rows of small raised bumps all over the paper, I assumed that this was the brail and he told me that it was. It just felt like a bunch of meaningless dots to me, and I had no clue what I was doing. I found out that learning Braille was pretty damn difficult.

161

I take my hat off to those who know how to do it. The problem I had was that I kept losing my place—my tongue would slide over the plastic so easily that I would end up in the wrong row of dots. I was constantly asking what this or that series of dots meant; after about an hour I was finally able to decipher one set of dots that formed the letter L, but that was as far as I got. In the end, I ended up learning a lot from the whole experience. Later, I would incorporate my own Braille symbols onto the buttons of my self-designed communication device.

Like I said, at the Courage Center I tried to keep busy. It helped pass the time. I wanted to go back to school, but I didn't know how since I was no longer able to read or write. I knew I wasn't stupid. I knew how to do everything before my accident, and I had learned many more things since. But now everything was so much harder, and I had to try and figure out how to do things in different ways. It was frustrating. They gave me an IQ test while I was there—I agreed to take it for I was curious what it would tell me about myself. I only remember two things about that test. First, I learned that I totally suck at doing math in my head. Second, I scored very high on the vocabulary portion. I began meeting with a teacher of sorts. I believe she tutored some of the residents who may have had learning disabilities, or those trying to get their GEDs. I wasn't sure. She asked me what I wanted to work on and I told her my spelling. That's all I could think of. Most everything else would require me to read or write, but I thought spelling was something

I could do in my head. Before my accident, in school for instance, I could usually figure out how to spell any word if I first wrote it down and looked at it. Or if all else failed, I would look it up in the dictionary. But now everything had changed, and I was no longer able to see to read, or use my hands to write. I would now have to learn how to do it all in my head. So she began quizzing me on how to spell certain words, like cat and ball. I know these are easy, don't laugh, but the words soon began to become more and more difficult. I felt like I was in a spelling bee. It was difficult for me, at times, to picture the words in my head in order to spell them. But at the same time it forced me to use my head to think, which was good.

Chapter Twenty-four

To See

Looking at the world through my blind eyes, I see the world from a new point of view. My senses are sharpened, and my hearing is acute. No longer do I have the luxury of judging people on how they look. Faces are lost in the shadows. Everyone looks the same through my eyes. I have learned sometimes beautiful people can be ugly and sometimes ugly people can be beautiful. It is how you perceive and not what you see, that's what matters. But often people's perceptions are clouded by ignorance and indifference. They often do not acknowledge what is right in front of them. Instead they turn away and they fail to see.

I didn't get many visitors while I was at the Courage Center. Once, a couple of my friends from home came to see me. My friend Dan that I used to go hunting and fishing with came to see me a couple of times. My mom's cousin Jack Olson and his wife spent an afternoon once with me as well, they were smart people. We walked along outside on the paths touring the grounds. At each bush or flower bed she would come to, Mrs. Olson would pause and recite the name of the flower or plant. Many of which I had never heard of before, I was impressed. Inside, I showed them my room, and then Jack wanted to go upstairs. Apparently he had spotted something on the roof of the building while driving up, and he wanted to check it out. So we took the elevator to the second floor, and he began his search. I had not spent a lot of time on the second floor, it was mostly offices. As Jack pushed me down the hall in my chair, rounding the corner he finally found what he was looking for. It was a small cramped room with a couple of small tables that were littered with electronic equipment. He explained to me how he had spotted the antennas on the roof that led to this room. I found out that this was a ham radio room.

Jack explained the difference between different types of ham radios, hf and vhf transceivers. He also told me that each operator of a ham radio has to pass a test before he can receive his call sign and license to talk. Each part of the country has a different code type prefix;

Minnesota's prefix was 00 for instance. He evidently knew a lot about radios.

One person who came back into my life at this time was my friend and former boss, Jack Vooge. He and his wife had been having some problems and were now divorcing. He told me about it when he came to visit me that fall. I felt bad for him and at the same time guilty because I had told him that I had seen his wife at the state fair a few weeks before. I thought he would be happy. What are the odds that in a crowd of thousands of people, I would bump into his wife? I wouldn't have noticed her if she had not called out to me. I guess she was shocked to see me there. It turned out that she had lied to Jack about where she was going, and went to the fair with her boyfriend instead. Anyway, it was news to him that I spotted his wife. I felt caught in the middle, wishing I had just kept my mouth shut. He told me that he was staying at his parents' house for the time being, until he found a place of his own. He took me to meet them in my van. They were very nice people. His dad was a very interesting fellow—he had been a frogman in World War II; I believe the frogmen were similar to the Navy Seals. After the war, he joined the local police department and one of his duties as an officer was as a rescue diver. He told me some crazy and gruesome stories about some of the dives he had been on. Jack had evidently heard all of his dad's stories about some of the dives he had been on, but I found them fascinating.

I spent Thanksgiving with Jack Vooge and his family. I hated the Courage Center; I don't think anyone enjoyed being there. So I took any excuse to leave I could find. Some people there didn't leave or go home for holidays. I felt sorry for those who had to stay behind. As for me, I tried to get out every chance I could get, be it going on outings, rock concerts or just sitting outside. I needed time to myself away from the Courage Center.

For Christmas that year I was able to fly home from Minnesota to Ohio where my family was now living. My older brother Jack drove down from his house in Brainerd to go with me. Flying on an airplane when you are disabled may be difficult, but not impossible. I have flown many times since my accident, both in commercial jets and also private planes with my uncle as pilot. The first time on a jet was going to be a new experience for me.

There are some things I have learned about flying that may be useful to disabled people who plan to travel by air. If you plan on bringing your wheelchair with you on the plane, you should first collapse it as much as possible, removing the footrest, seat cushion, and, depending on what kind of chair you have, you should also think about removing the backrest as well. I don't know what the rules are since September 11, but I would always carry these parts of my chair with me on the plane to prevent them from being broken or lost. I have had the baggage handlers break the footrest before, because I left them on the chair. Also, if you have a gel seat cushion and you leave it on your chair, it will freeze at thirty thousand feet. This could damage it, or at least take awhile to thaw out under your butt. Most wheelchairs can be reassembled in a matter of seconds.

Boarding the plane was also something new to me. They sort of loaded me up like a heavy piece of luggage. They seat-belted me into this special moving dolly that was equipped with a seat and about eight seat belts. There was no way I could have fallen out: I was trussed up like someone in a straitjacket! Once I was secure, two flight attendants tipped me back and pulled me up to the boarding ladder and down the aisle to my seat. Then after removing the seat belts, my brother helped transfer me over to my seat.

It felt kind of weird celebrating Christmas in a new, different house, but it was good to see everyone again, just the same. My parents' new house was not very wheelchair accessible. My dad and little brother had to carry me up a flight of stairs every time I had to use the toilet, since that's where the master bathroom was that had the largest doorway.

After about five days I had to return to the Courage Center and back to my routine of classes and therapies. Even though it was wintertime, I still tried to get out when I could. My friend Jack Vooge would come get me sometimes and we would drive around, sometimes stopping by the Mc Donald's Drive-Thru, other times Dairy Queen. I swear Jack was addicted to Mc Donald's cheeseburgers and chocolate malts from

Dairy Queen because he ate them all the time, even when I used to work for him.

Eventually winter retreated enough to allow spring to creep slowly forward. The dirty snow banks and ice melted, leaving behind pools and small rivers of cold, slushy water. Soon the first flowers of the year, tulips and daffodils, began to appear along with many of the songbirds that had flown south for the winter. Easter came and went. I had Easter dinner with Todd, one of the RA's, his fiancée, and his grandparents. had spent eight years in the army. I believe as a medic before moving back to Minnesota. He was a pretty nice guy.

A few of the RA's got married during my stay at the Courage Center. My friend Donald L and I went to one of the weddings. Her name was Jody, she was one of the RA's. Todd took off work to take us and he got in a little trouble when he brought us home drunk.

I was going to have to find a place to live once I got out of the Courage Center. I had never had a place of my own before, and I wasn't exactly sure where to start. Luckily there were people there to help with that kind of stuff, like finding apartments and setting up bank accounts. One of which was a woman named Amy S.

There was an organization called Accessible Space Incorporated (ASI). They provided low-income accessible housing for people with disabilities. They owned apartment buildings throughout Minnesota, North and South Dakota, and I think a few other states as well. Before my accident I remember reading in the newspaper when I lived at home how they were building an apartment building for the disabled in Brainerd, Minnesota. I remember thinking to myself that it was a different idea to make an apartment building totally accessible and exclusive to people with disabilities. I also thought it was a good idea, not knowing that in a little over a year's time I would be living in one of those buildings.

Amy S. took me to meet with someone from the ASI office where I was put on a waiting list for an apartment. They asked me a bunch of questions. One of which was where did I want to live? I told them Brainerd, for I knew that town having gone to school there, also because I had family there. My brother Jack, and later my sister Aimee, moved to Brainerd as well. But it turned out that the building in Brainerd was full and there were no vacant apartments. So I had to think of somewhere else to live. They told me of a brand-new building that had just been built in Saint Cloud, Minnesota, which was an hour away from Brainerd. So I filled out an application for a two-bedroom apartment. I had asked Deann to move in with me, partly because I was dumb and naïve not wanting to live alone, also because I still needed help.

My discharge date was set for the first week in June. I had a lot to do before then. My parents sent me the money that I had saved before I was admitted to the Courage Center— around nine hundred dollars, which Amy S. helped me deposit into my checking account. Then armed with my checkbook, I went shopping. The one thing that I wanted to buy for myself after a year of sleeping on a hard narrow hospital bed was a decent, big, comfortable bed. So my friend Jack Vooge took me to a furniture store to buy a bed. I found out that furniture wasn't cheap, and beds were no exception. After testing several mattresses, I found a queen-size bed I liked, and it was on sale. I asked the sales person how long the bed would be on sale for. She told me just a few more days. My discharge was still not for a couple more weeks, so the sales person agreed to hold on to the bed and store it until I was ready to pick it up, granted I pay for it now. So I wrote her a check for the price of the bed, which was close to six hundred dollars. But when it came time for me to move and pick up my bed from the furniture store, they informed me that they no longer had my bed; they had sold it. I was pissed and I wanted some answers, but no one had any answers for me. I was set to move to Saint Cloud the next day and I had nowhere to sleep. Those crooked people at the furniture store had stolen my money, and had sold my bed. Hearing what had happened the recreational therapist agreed to let me have an old twin-size bed that she was trying to get rid of.

I found out that the Courage Center was charging my insurance company over two hundred dollars a day for me to stay there. I could have stayed in a hotel and lived off room service for cheaper. I was pretty angry, and thought I was being taken advantage of, so I decided to take a few things with me when I moved. I thought "why not let the Courage Center help me to furnish my new apartment." So with Deann's help I stuffed two of my moving boxes full of towels, sheets, blankets, wash cloths, pillows, and pillowcases. Though it may have been a bit of thievery on my part, this small act of rebellion sure felt good. The final irony was having the staff of the Courage Center help me load the contraband boxes into my van. They had no clue what was in them. I had just spent a difficult year of my life in this place, vowing to never return as a patient. In spite of myself and even though I hated this whole place at times, I still broke down and cried when I left.

Chapter Twenty-five

Heathen

If you open your eyes, it is plain to see,

That there is no place for a heathen like me.

I am on my own, all alone,

As I think back to when my life went bad.

My friends have all moved away,

Some of my friends are dead,

Some of my friends are in prison, it has been said.

The things that I want, I know I will never have.

The freedom that I crave will never happen,

So I do what I can do.

I drink a lot of whiskey and I got some tattoos.

I am too smart for my own good.

Nobody understands me; they never could.

I want so badly to just pick up and leave,

But where would I go?

I don't know.

There is no place for a heathen like me.

I was nineteen years old and ready to live on my own. I guess it was an accomplishment of sorts, since two year before I was in a coma on death's door. The doctors told my parents that I would never wake up, and if I did I would be a vegetable for the rest of my life. I had just moved into my first apartment by myself. That just goes to show that doctors don't always know everything. My apartment was on the third floor at the end of the hall. The name of the apartment building was Quarry Heights, no doubt because it was built near one of the local granite quarries. It was an assisted living facility, meaning, in most cases, that there was someone there twenty-four hours a day to assist those who needed help. In this way people with disabilities were able to live independently in their own homes. I would live there for a year until an apartment opened up in Brainerd. My parents and little brother Jed drove up from Ohio to help me move. After helping me move in, my family left for a week to visit my brother Jack in Brainerd. When they returned, they brought a new bed with them, which was very nice and a heck of a lot better than the bed I was given.

Living on my own was a new experience. I now had bills to pay, and I had to figure out a way to get groceries. The nearest stores were a mile away. I did not have my power wheelchair yet, and the aides were not allowed to drive my van. But I found out that Saint Cloud had a metro bus line that was equipped with wheelchair lifts and tie downs. The fare was about seventy cents one-way, so I took the bus most places: like to the grocery store, out to eat, and even to the bar. I had grown my hair long at the Courage Center, and after I moved I grew a mustache and goatee. I thought it made me look older. Maybe it did, because I never got carded.

Deann still had another month or two left at the Courage Center before she could join me in Saint Cloud. So in the meantime, I was sort of stuck in my apartment. I did not have my power wheelchair yet, so I wasn't able to get around my apartment and push the call button if I had to. So I had the aides rig up a long piece of string tying one end to the call switch and the other end to my hand. This worked pretty well. Also, some of the aides that worked there would stop in and check on me from time to time. Most of the aides who worked there were pretty cool. But after awhile people got married, moved away, or found different jobs.

The building was set up using a system of shared services. This meant that the residents had to share the aides' time with the other residents, as opposed to having a private agency, which a couple of other residents had. It was a pretty good arrangement, except for the fact that there were one or two residents who were constantly pushing their call lights.

After Deann moved in, things changed and I found out how difficult it sometimes can be to live with another person. When you live with someone, you find out things that maybe you didn't want to know and you would be better off not knowing. I admit I was a bit naïve at the time when it came to relationships, but so was she. Though I was thankful for the help she gave me, there were times when she became very hard to live with. I guess in the end everything has a price.

Saint Cloud was a college town that had a lot of good restaurants and bars. It could be a fun place to live and for a kid like me, unsupervised and away from home and I got into a bit of trouble. A lot of the residents at the building were younger people, who Deann and I would drink and party with. One of these was a friend of mine from the Courage Center named Chad. He had broken his neck in a car accident and was now living in an apartment across town. Deann and I would take the bus to the bar. Deann and I would often take one or two of the aides from the building with us. Then we, some of the residents from the building and my friend Chad would all meet at the bar. The aides didn't mind getting out away from the building for a few hours. They would help us who were in wheelchairs to the bathroom and with bringing drinks to the table. It got to be pretty fun, but one night I drank so much that it put an end to my drinking days for awhile. I drank so much that night; all in all I had seven or eight different kinds of alcohol, which was more than I could handle. I still weighed around 114 pounds at the time. I didn't think I was that drunk, but ten minutes later I was throwing up in the alley behind the bar. I think I had an allergic reaction to the Jagermeister, which I had never had before. In any case,

I was now violently ill thanks to my own stupidity. But it turned out that my stupidity knew no bounds for I was sick throwing up for the next three days before being admitted to the hospital.

Once at the hospital the first thing they did was pump my stomach. I tried to tell them that there was nothing in there since I had been puking for days, but they went ahead and did it anyway. Having your stomach pumped is a freaky and very unpleasant experience; I don't recommend it. They shoved a long rubber tube up my nose and down my throat; I was then made to swallow it choking and gagging as they slid the tube down my throat and into my stomach. After that, I believe they hooked the other end up to a machine that I think flushed my stomach with some kind of liquid the same time sucked the liquid back up through the tube in my nose. I think it was a little like that water suction tool that the dentist uses. The only difference was this tool was shoved down my nose. The cool liquid made me feel better briefly but I had been dry heaving for the past few days where nothing would come up except for mouthfuls of bitter brown bile. I was very dehydrated and also in a great deal of pain, which, I later learned, was due to an inflamed pancreas. Also, my kidneys were starting to shut down as well. I didn't know how bad off I was, but the doctor told me that in another day or two and I could have died. I was a little shook-up by that news. All this pain and sickness from one night of drinking was a bit of a wake-up call for me to slow down. I was smart enough to realize how stupid and lucky I had been. Unfortunately, it took having my stomach pumped to see it. I spent the next week in the hospital and the next month recovering from the whole ordeal. While in the hospital, my friends came to visit along with many of the aides that worked at the apartment building. They had me on morphine for the pain, so I spent most of the time sleeping. There was a question about the bar getting in trouble for serving me since I was a minor, but I didn't want to press any charges. I knew what I was doing. The only one I could blame was my own stupid ass. Needless to say, I did not return to that bar. When my parents found out that I was in the hospital and why, they were worried and upset . I felt like shit for upsetting them.

While living in Saint Cloud I finally received my first power wheelchair. I now had the freedom and mobility to get around and go places by myself. I wanted to try to go back to school. A few of the aides that worked at the buildings were going to school at Saint Cloud State. One of them, his name was Tim, took me on his day off to check out the campus. He showed me around to several of the buildings. He took me to the building that housed the English department, for that's what I was interested in. As he pushed me toward the front door, I did my best to memorize my surroundings to see if it would be possible to get around there by myself. There was a ramp leading to the front door. I think there was a button to open it, but it was out of reach. Once inside we took the elevator to the second floor, and went down a hall, through a small narrow doorway and into one of the classrooms. I knew then that I would not be able to negotiate the obstacles like elevators and doors by myself. I would need to have help, not only getting around but also help taking notes. Unfortunately, I was not able to take one of the aides from the building with me to help, nor was I able to take the bus by myself and call them to pick me up. My plans to go back to school would have to be put on hold for the next few years until I would be able to try again.

Chapter Twenty-six

Common Ground

Walking down this lonely road,

The world looks different through my blind eyes.

All of the familiar landmarks are long gone.

I don't know which way to turn,

I try to see through the darkness and haze

That clouds my vision and dims my gaze.

Sometimes it's hard to get around,

When you can't find any common ground.

I close my eyes and I am swallowed in a well of memories,

Of a time when I was whole, when I could see.

Walking through the forest,

Striding amongst the trees

With the sun on my face, speckled and dappled through the leaves.

Or I could be walking along the beach, my bare toes sinking in the

warm sand,

The wind off the lake is in my hair, and there is a bottle of whiskey in

my hand.

But those times are in the past, the wood and the water are no more.

The places that I knew so well are gone,

I have to start over once again.

Trying to figure out how I ended up here in this town,

So far from home and my common ground.

After a year of living in Saint Cloud, a two-bedroom apartment opened at the ASI apartment building in Brainerd. My parents once again drove up from Ohio to help me move. This time Deann moved with me as well. Saint Cloud was okay but I wanted a change. I wanted to find some common ground, someplace where I was familiar with the streets and places I once knew. Brainerd was a town I knew. In addition to having family there, things were also a bit more convenient. There was a grocery store across the street from the apartment along with a small strip mall about a half a block away. There were also a few restaurants within walking distance, a movie rental place, and a couple of parks as well.

My apartment in Brainerd was also on the third floor across the hall from the laundry room. There was one home care company that provided home health care services to most of the residents in the building, including Deann and I. It has been my experience that some home care companies will be very nice to you at first, then after a few months their commitment and services will start to decline and any promises regarding your care will be forgotten.

Good Heart was one example of this. I believe there were some questionable accounting practices associated with that company. In any case, I think they lost the contract to provide services for our building and eventually went out of business. Home health care is a multi-million dollar industry where the home care agencies, depending on their number of clients, can take in huge profits during the course of a year. But sadly, it also has one of the highest turnover rates of any job. This is due to the low wages and lack of benefits that most home care companies fail to provide for their employees. Granted, there are other factors that may play into the high turnover rate, such as the price of gas and other work-related expenses.

Deann and I stayed with Good Heart for two years before they went out of business and we were forced to find a new home care agency. This was something new for me—before, I had just used whatever company was in place at the apartments. It had been convenient and reassuring to know someone was there twenty-four hours a day if I needed help.

But there were drawbacks as well. Good Heart did not allow their aides to drive. This meant that if I wanted to go anywhere, like the library for instance, I had to take the city bus, which was called Dial-a-Ride. That got to be expensive, not to mention a pain in the butt. Though I think the fair was only seventy-five cents one way, I had to take an aide with me and pay for their fair as well. Also, if I wanted to go to the other side of town, the price of the fair would be doubled. Another drawback of riding the bus was that it shut down at 5 PM, opposed to about 10:30 PM for the buses in Saint Cloud.

If you or someone you know is planning to hire a home care agency, there are some questions that might be helpful to ask as all home care agencies are different. Some are better than others, so you should find out as much as possible about a company before you hire them. Don't just pick the first one you see in the phone book; you need to do your homework and ask questions. Keep in mind that their priorities should be helping you first and making a profit second, but sadly that is not always the case. You need to remember that the home care agency is working for you: you are in charge. Also, the aides that are sent to your home are there to assist you with homemaking, housekeeping, and skilled nursing tasks; they are not there to be your personal slaves to order around.

With that said, here are a few questions that might be useful to ask when searching for a home care agency. First, ask how large the company is and how long they have been in business. Sometimes small home care companies have a hard time with staffing if two or more of their employees happen to get sick. Second, find out if they are licensed and bonded—make sure they are legit and not some sort of scam. Third, ask what qualifications, training, and experience the aides are required to have for their job. Some home care agencies will hire just about anyone, which can be scary not to mention not very safe. So if possible, you should look for an agency that requires their aides to be licensed and trained with qualifications such as STNA, which stands for state tested nursing assistant.

Deann and I chose a home care agency named Bannertrust. One of the reasons we chose them was that their aides were allowed to drive, so

I no longer had to take the bus or remain stuck at home. I now had the freedom to go places. And it so happened that many of the aides that once worked for Good Heart now worked for Bannertrust. This turned out to be good and bad. It was good in the sense that we knew many of them from before, and it was bad because one of the aides turned out to be a con artist and thief. She stole my wallet twice, emptying it of cash and even my book of stamps. But I was able to recover my wallet both times: once over a fence in a neighbor's yard, and another time under the lining of a box of potato chips that was in the office at the apartments.

People have stolen my money before. It happened at the Courage Center, in Saint Cloud, and now again in Brainerd. I guess because they knew I could not see, they thought they could help themselves to my things, figuring I would not notice anything missing. Just because I was blind did not make me stupid, for it is pretty hard to not realize when your wallet is missing. I did everything I was supposed to do; I reported it to the home care office and even filled out a police report. I told them whom I suspected, but since I didn't see her take it there was no proof, so nothing happened and she was allowed to continue to work and to steal from the other residents in the building.

I was not the only one she stole from. She talked Deann into buying a ring for her with the promise of making the payments. She made up some story about her credit. She also stole some books from Deann after signing her up for a book club without her knowledge. She stole money and a bottle of pain pills from a quadriplegic that lived on the floor below me; he wasn't able to get out of bed to see what she was doing. She eventually got caught when she stole a diamond wedding ring from one of the residents and sold it to a pawnshop using her son's name and ID. Since the ring was appraised at over five hundred dollars, it was a felony and she had to go to jail. She pleaded no contest to the charges, and was sentenced to two months in jail. When she got out she was forced to pay restitution, so I got some of my money back. She lost her job and was banned from working in the health care field. Part of me was glad she got punished, and part of me felt sorry for her. She managed to fool a lot of people with her lies before she got caught, including me.

During my years in Brainerd, I was stolen from quite a bit. I had my medicine taken twice. Other things that were stolen include: CDs, food and alcohol, clothes, cash, change for the Laundromat, and even my yearbook. Most of these things were taken by dishonest aides who were being paid to take care of me. Each time it would happen, I would report it to the home care agency, foolishly thinking they would do something about it, but they never did.

I did not want to fill out a police report because I felt there was nothing they could do; also, because I did not want to worry my parents. When my wallet was stolen the first time, I filled out a police report and had to go to the courthouse and DMV to replace my ID, as a result my name was in the newspaper. My parents heard about it, all the way down in Ohio and were very upset.

Living with Deann and trying to deal with my home health aides could be very trying at times. She was a jealous person who could be selfish and mean at times. If there was an aide that I got along with and that I liked, Deann would call the office and tell them she didn't want them. And since we had to share the same aide, the agency would pull them out. Granted, not everyone is going to get along with everyone else, but her petty selfish games used to really piss me off. She did not realize that people were working to pay bills, or to buy food for their kids. I don't think she ever stopped to think how her actions affected others at the time.

There was one resident, named Suzy, who had ALS (or Lou Gehrig's disease), she could not move or speak, but her mind was perfectly intact. She communicated by using an alphabet board—a piece of paper with the alphabet printed on it. She had a hard time with new aides because many of them did not take the time or have the patience to listen to her. Instead, many of them would ignore her or treat her like a baby, which would piss her off and she would tell them to get the hell out. After awhile Bannertrust got sick of Deann complaining, Suzy kicking people out, and my being stolen from. So they told us from that point on we, could find our own help. Thankfully Deann and I knew enough of the aides to put together a loose schedule, but Suzy wasn't as lucky.

Bannertrust refused to care for her anymore. She was forced to move to a different ASI building in Duluth, Minnesota, where no one knew her or how to take proper care of her. Less than two months later she was dead, and I feel that Bannertrust's actions may have contributed to her death.

I don't know if what Bannertrust was doing to us was legal. We were doing their job for them by calling people to ask them to work to fill our own schedules and they were getting paid for it. I didn't know how they stayed in business. One of their employees who worked for us also worked in the office. She would fill out fraudulent time sheets and then turn them in. Since she had access to the payroll and computer records, nothing was done about it. Either Bannertrust didn't know about it or they didn't care. They were putting profits first and helping their clients second. It was just another form of dishonesty and thievery that I had to contend with. Not everyone who worked for Bannertrust was bad; there were a few employees who truly enjoyed helping others. One of those was, surprisingly, the wife of Bannertrust's owner. The company was co-owned by a brother and sister, and the brother's wife (I believe her name was Brenda) used to fill in as an aide from time to time. She worked in the office of an orthopedic surgeon during the day and used to fill in occasionally some nights and weekends. She was a very kind and compassionate person—nothing like her sister-in-law or her husband.

Chapter Twenty-seven

Second Chance

I have killed and I have healed.

I have been killed and I have been healed.

The secret of life is so simple,

But it takes a lifetime to understand.

I have passed through the shadow of death,

And now I am a very different man.

I ran out of time, I missed my flight,

I missed the dance, but I'm still alive and now I have a second chance

at life.

A second chance to try and help people.

I want them to know how it feels; I want them to understand.

I may not walk: instead, I now use a chair of steel,

But I am still just a man.

I had a second chance to travel, a second chance to move.

A second chance to come here, and write this for you. I had been frustrated trying to think of some way to communicate. My speech was still difficult to understand at times. I was going to speech therapy and occupational therapy while I was living in Brainerd: I was still trying to get my hands and speech to work. If I could just get either one to work, I knew it would be a lot easier to try to communicate. In occupational therapy, they ordered and built hand braces for me to wear. After wearing them for an hour or more, they would become painful. Because I was not able to take them off by myself, so I designed a Velcro release that would allow me to take them off with my teeth. Unfortunately, the braces did not loosen up the contractures in my wrists enough to allow me the use of my hands. I even underwent two separate and painful appointments to receive Botox injections into the muscles of my forearms. Botox is a toxic poison; it's a form of food poising called botulism. In minute amounts it is sometimes used in cosmetic surgery to remove the appearance of wrinkles.

I had been given some information and literature about a doctor in Saint Cloud who was using Botox injections to relieve pain and spasticity in people who had suffered accidents, or were suffering from other ailments. He was reported to have had some limited success with a few patients. I was willing to try anything to fix my hands. I received about eight of the shots over the course of my two visits. The shots did seem to work a little bit; my wrists loosened up slightly for a few days.

Then, after about a week, the effects wore off and my muscles and my wrist would tighten back up once again. It became very frustrating for me. I knew I was smart and I also knew how to take apart and fix many things, but try as I might, I was not able to fix myself. I had to accept the fact that I would never regain the use of my hands, but I didn't have to like it.

I also focused on improving my speech without much success. This was a constant source of self-consciousness and frustration for me. Once again, here was another problem I could not fix. My speech remained soft and at times hard to understand. I needed a way to communicate, because Goddamn it, I had a lot to say. I started thinking of some way I could possibly type, but without the use of my hands I knew this would be a problem. Not to mention I was now blind and unable to read or see any kind of keyboard. I had to think. If there was no way to see a keyboard, then perhaps there may be a way to feel one. I remembered when I was in high school, before my accident, I would type up homework assignments and reports on an electric Smith Corona typewriter. I remember that this model had raised dots or little bumps on the keys that I assumed must be Braille. If I could memorize the layout and the keyboard and different bumps on the keys, then maybe I could use my tongue to type. It was a crazy idea, but I was going to give it a try. So I went looking for a typewriter. I went to several different stores that sold typewriters, but I was unable to find one that had the bumps on the keys. Apparently those models had been discontinued. Being stubborn and unwilling to give up so easily, I bought one anyway. It was a lot bigger than I remembered and with no way to tell the keys apart, I was hopelessly confused. I needed a way to mark the keys so I could distinguish them from one another. So I bought a label-making gun, one of those kinds where you turn a dial and pull a trigger to imprint letters or numbers onto a strip of plastic tape. I thought it was a good idea and it should have worked but for the fact that the labels I made kept falling off the keys. I finally concluded that this wasn't going to work and I was going to have to think of something else to try.

I began using my mind and started thinking of different ways to write and communicate. The question was how I was going to manage to overcome three separate disabilities: my blindness, my inability to use my hands, and, the biggest stumbling block of all, my speech. The problem or challenge now became how do you create or build something without using your hands and just your mind.

I had to think of what kind of devices were available for someone like me with multiple disabilities that would allow me to write and communicate. It was like that line from that old movie *Cool Hand Luke*: "What we have here is a failure to communicate," that was me. As far as I knew, such a device did not exist or no one had invented one yet. The more I thought the more my mind kept straying to the idea of a computer. But I dismissed the thought. For one thing, how could someone like me possibly operate a computer? Secondly, I knew next to nothing about computers. But the idea, like a persistent itch that you cannot reach to scratch would not go way.

Then I started thinking about how people communicated before telephones, fax machines, and computers. How did cave men communicate and send messages to one another? Perhaps they would beat on a drum or a hollow log. What about the Indians? Well in the movies they would use smoke signals to send messages like some secret code. Then I thought, how did the people who settled the country communicate with one another and write and send messages to one another? I thought they used the telegraph and Morse code. Maybe, just maybe, I could use Morse code to write.

A few days later, I was over at my brother Jack's house. My brother Jack is a computer whiz, or at least I thought so. I knew hardly anything about computers at the time. He had a voice-recognition typing program that he wanted me to try out; he had seen some of my frustrations with trying to communicate, and he thought this program might help. He had a small microphone attached to his computer that I was to speak into. I was to say words into the microphone, and in turn it was supposed to print my words onto the computer screen. Unfortunately, my voice was so soft at the time, and the microphone had difficulty registering it. I did manage to say a few words loud and clear enough for the microphone to pick up, but I also had many more mistakes. It was a good idea, and I was frustrated and disappointed when it did not work.

Most people take the ability to speak and communicate for granted, but as for me it would be one of the hardest challenges I would have to try to overcome. Sitting there with my brother, I suggested trying something else. That idea I had for using Morse code to type had been rattling around in my head for a few days now, so I decided to run it past my brother to see what he thought of it. I asked if he could let me try something, he said sure. After explaining my idea, I wanted to demonstrate possibly how it would work. So, leaning over in my wheelchair I clicked the buttons on his computer mouse with my tongue. He said it was a good idea but his computer mouse only had three buttons. He didn't know if it would be possible to reprogram a computer mouse and to make it run a whole computer with only three buttons, so I told him to use more buttons. Maybe there was a way to wire a bunch of computer mice together? He told me that he would think about it.

In the meantime, I began learning and teaching myself Morse code. I checked out a book on Morse code from the library, and every day I had my home health aides quiz me on the different letters and symbols. After two weeks, I returned the book having memorized the Morse code alphabet, punctuation, and numbers zero through ten.

I had no idea if what I wanted or what I was thinking about would even be possible, to invent a way to write with Morse code. I didn't yet know how I was going to figure it out, just that somehow it had to be possible. So as a joke, I had one of my home health aides help me write out a letter to my parents in Morse code. They had no idea what it said and my mom had to break out her encyclopedias to translate it; I thought that was pretty funny. Then I wrote a letter to my Uncle Bill also in Morse code. He was pretty good at crossword puzzles, so I wanted to see if he could figure out what it said. I don't think he ever did, but what he did do was show my letter to some people, one of whom turned out to be a guy named Tom who was an inventor of sorts. He was intrigued by my situation and after talking to my brother Jack about using my idea of Morse code to type he agreed to build me a switch that I could operate with my tongue. He also offered to give me an old computer he had laying around. My idea was for a switch that I could operate with my tongue, which I could use to type Morse code, and somehow have the dots and dashes be translated into text or words onto the computer screen. I had a blueprint in my head of what the switch should look like, and when I got it, I found it to be very close to what I had pictured in my head.

The material for the switch box was made of a bulletproof Plexiglas called Lexan that housed ten microswitch buttons that my brother Jack later soldered into a length of printer cable. He then soldered and wired the cable into a video game controller that he then plugged into the game port of my computer. It may have been homemade and a bit crude, but I was going to do my best to make it work. It turned out the switch was only half the equation, for Jack first needed to write the software program to run the Morse code switch. I named the program Virtual Morse, and since this was a homemade prototype device that no one to our knowledge had ever tried before, he had to make it up as he went along. The first version of the program was pretty basic. After determining what buttons I wanted for each function, he started writing the program. He used the sounds of an arcade pinball computer game to add sound effects to the buttons, so I could tell where I was. I now had a button for the dot and one for the dash to type Morse code. I also had a button for space and one for enter. The most amazing part of it was that the thing actually worked. I was now able to type words with my tongue using Morse code.

For the next version of the program, my brother Jack recorded his own voice for the letters of the alphabet. He used the phonetic or military alphabet which was a little confusing at first. For instance let's say I wanted to type the word **cat**. Instead of thinking C A T, I would have to think **Charlie alpha tango,** which was -.-. .- - . This was very slow and time-consuming at first, and I remember thinking that this was going to take me a hundred years to write anything. But I soon began to improve my typing speed with practice. Also, my brother Jack would help me update and make changes to the program. He helped me add new functions to the keys, such as the ability to save or delete my work. I was now able to have the computer read back to me what I had written. Eventually Jack would add the ability to send and receive e-mail to the program as well, all with only ten buttons and by using my tongue.

Chapter Twenty-eight

Black

I have that feeling again,

It comes and it goes.

It's like an emptiness, a blackness: a sadness.

It's in my head,

It's in my soul.

I can't seem to shake off these black thoughts.

Am I going crazy, am I cracking up?

Or am I just too sane to go insane?

I try to be happy on the outside,

But the feeling remains

As if I am dying inside.

It went away when I was with you,

But now that you are gone it's been creeping slowly back.

It's a heaviness that weighs upon my heart.

It makes me feel hollow;

It makes me feel black.

I don't know what to do.

I am feeling lost without you.

I wish that you would come back,

So my world won't be so black.

The year was now 1997. I had now been disabled for five years. I was living in an apartment in Brainerd, Minnesota working on learning to write again when I received the disturbing news that my brother Jason had committed suicide. Growing up we were very close. Our birthdays were eleven months and three days apart, so for three days of the year we would both be the same age. My mom always said it was like having twins the hard way.

He had moved to Ohio with my parents and two younger brothers after selling the house in Minnesota. Then, after my brother Ben finished high school, he and Jason set out for Alaska. Ben was enrolled at the university, and Jason planned to stay with friends and work. Alaska is a land of extremes. During the early spring and summer the sun often never sets in places. The sun shines nearly twenty-four hours a day in most places, but during the winter months it is dark and often very cold. Depending on where you are in the state, there is often little or no sunlight for weeks at a time. The cold temperatures, in excess of sixty below in places, combined with a lack of daylight often have a negative effect on people. I believe that may have been what had affected my brother. After two years in Alaska, he returned to Ohio, but I don't think he was ever the same. I had once read that Alaska has the highest rate of alcoholism and suicide per capita of any state. Upon returning to Ohio, my brother Jason began to slip into a depression. My parents took him to a doctor who prescribed him some medication, but this did little to help and may have possibly made things worse. He began sleeping all the time and when he would awake he would eat. This was not like him. My brother Jason had always been a trim, fit, and active guy, but with his continuous sleeping from the drugs he was taking, along with the eating and lack of exercise, it all began to take a toll on his waistline. He went from a size thirty-two waist all the way to a size forty in a matter of months. I sent him a box of movies and some books on tape to cheer him up and help to take his mind off of things, for we were both big movie buffs. I just felt so helpless, and I wanted to do something, anything, to help him. Another one of the side effects of the medication that my brother was taking or possibly when he wasn't taking it was that he began to hear voices. Then one night when my parents were not home, my kind, funny, gentle, compassionate brother listened to the voices. He drove down a dark, lonely country road away from the house and took his own life.

My Uncle Carl flew my brother Jack and me down to Ohio in his plane for the funeral. I wrote my brother Jason's eulogy for the funeral service. I believe that was the hardest thing I ever had to write, but I thought I owed it to him, as my way of saying good-bye. My Brother Jason's body was cremated and my dad sprinkled his ashes over a waterfall near his house, for he always liked that place.

Losing a loved one is never easy. No parent should ever have to bury their own child. My mom took my Brother Jason's death exceptionally hard. Our whole family was in mourning and saddened by the unexpected loss of our brother, cousin, nephew, grandson, and son for he was all of these things. My brother Jason had his whole life ahead of him, but would now remain twenty-three forever.

After returning to Minnesota, I didn't know what to do. I just wanted to be left alone, which is nearly impossible when you live in an apartment building. The walls are thin and everyone wants to know your business. I hated that. I did my best to keep to myself. After Deann and I switched home care agencies, I persuaded her to move out to an apartment on the first floor. I just could not live with her anymore. There were a lot of little reasons, and over time they seemed to add up. The fights and arguments were part of it. But I think we both needed our own space. I was fed up with people, and I just wanted to be alone. I needed to find a quiet place to get away, so I began going to the cemetery every day. That was one place I knew that was void of the constant noise of people. It was five blocks away. I would drive there in my power chair. Once there, I would follow the paths to a far secluded spot under the shady canopy of an ancient knurled burr oak tree.

There in that quiet place under the tree with no other sounds except for the birds in the trees and the silence of the souls who were all around me, I would open the dam to my heart and weep. My emotions welling and surging like a flood overflowing the Twin Rivers of my eyes. I would give into my grief so naked and painfully raw, like a fresh wound upon my shattered soul, and I would weep for the brother I would never see again. For hours upon end I was helpless to do anything else but weep. Day after day, I would return to that quiet spot beneath the shady boughs of the tree to pour my heart out all of the anger and crushing grief that was pent-up inside me. I would let loose, soaking the ground in a flood of hot, salty tears. I would sit there in that beautiful, tranquil place and I would curse God, for there was no one else to blame. Why was I spared and allowed to live while my brother was allowed to die? Why couldn't it have been me who died? Why, why, why goddamn you, why not me? Why! I would weep and curse for hours until I had no more tears left in my body left to shed. Then, with my grief spent, I would go home only to return the following day.

I didn't know what to do to ease my grief. Nothing seemed to help. I tried getting drunk, but eventually the whiskey always wore off. I was just so tired of the pain and grief—I just wanted it to end. My thoughts were very black then and I began to think about taking my own life. I just wanted to end the pain. That's when the irony of my situation really sank in. What if I ended up worse off than I was already? How the fuck does one kill themselves if they can't use their hands. I began to laugh at the cruel absurdity of it all. To quote Hamlet, "Thus conscience does make cowards of us all."

Something happened to me during this time, something I cannot explain. I was sitting in my secluded spot under the tree in the cemetery and had finished weeping and cursing for the day, but when I went to leave, I found that I could not move. I had somehow gotten off the path and was now stuck. I tried moving forward, then in reverse, but with no luck. I changed gears and tried the same thing in high speed, but still with no luck. My chair had fourteen-inch knobby tires with pretty good tread, so I was able to go most places, even through snow, but for some reason I seemed to be stuck. I tried and tried to get free.

I tried shifting my weight from side to side in my chair in an attempt to break free from whatever was holding me fast. I tried everything I could think of to get free, even yelling for help. But I was far from any main paths and my dry, parched voice did not carry vary far. I tried my chair over and over until I smelt burning rubber. Then I gave up and just sat. I thought I knew what had happened; one of the roots from the tree had probably gotten snagged on one of the wheelie bars on my chair (wheelie bars are a small set of wheels that are attached to the back of the wheelchair to prevent it from flipping backwards). I was hopelessly stuck way off and far away from the main path and any living soul. The cemetery was fairly large and thickly wooded in places. There was a steep, sloping bluff on one end that led down to the Mississippi River. This was covered in trees and all kinds of thick, choking brush. I sat near the bluff a hundred yards or so from the main path and waited for the hours to creep slowly by. I could hear the bells sound from the courthouse or from some church every hour, for sound carried surprisingly well over the river in that quiet place. In any case, I was able to tell and keep track of time. That was a small comfort to me.

As the hours and minutes slipped by so agonizingly slow, I started to become aware that the sun was starting to set. I heard the bells for 7 o'clock then 7:30; this was followed by the bells for 8 o'clock, 8:30, 9 o'clock and 9:30. By this time it was fairly dark and hard to see. My vision was still very poor—it was a lot like looking under water, very fuzzy and out of focus. I got around by remembering where I had been, also by driving by sound and also by feel. This was a bit rough on my footrest, for I tended to run into stuff from time to time.

The shadows began to pool beneath the silent, dark trees. Then the blackness would slowly spread outwards, rolling to cover the ground like a black tide. I wondered if anyone would ever find me. Would the crows lead people to my remains in the days ahead? How long would it take for me to succumb to dehydration and the elements? These thoughts went through my mind as I prepared myself for the long, cold night ahead. These thoughts were no doubt fueled by the idea of spending a night or two in the cemetery.

I wasn't afraid of the dark, but I thought the prospect of spending the night camping out in the graveyard might be a bit ghoulish and a tad creepy. Let's just say there were more attractive places that I would have preferred to spend the night at. I had just closed my eyes for a few minutes in preparation of the long night ahead and the far-off dawn, when I heard a noise some ways behind me. My eyes flew open and I was instantly wide-awake. I craned my head around trying to peer into the gathering gloom, my ears straining to hear over the thundering and pounding of my heart. I was startled, more than anything, to hear a sound after so many hours of silence. It was a smack, smack, smack sound that took me a moment or two to place. It was the sound of running feet, of someone running in sneakers over pavement or hard-packed earth. I didn't know where it was coming from. There was only one other gate on this end that was always kept locked, the hinges nearly rusted shut. But as I sat there in the growing darkness, I realized the footsteps were growing louder as the running figure drew near. My mind was racing to process what I was hearing and, later, what I was seeing; it didn't make sense. Who in their right mind would be jogging through a cemetery at night when there was a well-lit sidewalk that ran along the outside of the cemetery? Moreover, of all the paths, the one I sat on dead-ended after twenty yards or so. The person coming up behind me would have had to cut through the cemetery without tripping over headstones in the fading light. To this day I still have no explanation for what happened next, nor have I told people about it. I was trying to look behind me to see who or what was coming. Then all of a sudden a large figure ran out behind the tree and into view.

I was startled once again to see what appeared to be a large, tall man run out from behind the tree. He appeared to be dressed in some kind of jogging attire. On his feet he wore what looked like brand new, white tennis shoes or sneakers. The rest of him seemed to be wearing a dark colored sweat suit that may have been gray or possibly red. The light was fading fast by this time, so I wasn't able to get a very clear look at the figure for the few brief moments it was visible to me. The one thing that I do remember about the figure is the sweatband that it wore; it was very white and new-looking—the same as the shoes. You can believe me or not, I am just trying to explain to you what it was that I saw. As the figure ran past me on the trail I called after it in a dry, parched whisper of a voice to help me. To my astonishment, the figure stopped dead in its tracks as if it had actually heard my whispered cries for help. There was no way anyone could have heard my voice from more than a few inches away, but the runner who was now twenty yards ahead on the trail seemed to have heard me.

I watched as the figure ran towards me, and assumed it was going to stop in front of me, but to my astonishment it ran right past me and kept on going down the path out of view. I yelled after it to stop, I was stuck. By this time I was becoming a bit frantic and also pissed-off that someone could just leave me sit there. The figure had to have seen me, as I was just a few feet off the path. I didn't know what to think. How could someone abandon a person in the middle of a deserted graveyard at night? That's what I thought anyway, but all of a sudden I felt my chair being wrestled onto the path. There was someone behind me, pushing and lifting up the back end of the chair to clear the tree root. An average power chair weighs two to three hundred pounds empty, so whoever was behind me had to be fairly strong. I yelled to them to hold on and wait a minute, I had to put my chair in gear first. With all the pushing and shaking, I wasn't able to reach the head controls for my chair. Once I got my chair going and I was back on the path, I turned to thank the jogger for helping me. But as I turned my chair around to look back and say thank you, my mouth fell open in stunned silence for there was no one there. All the hair rose on the back of my neck. I turned around and got the hell out of there as fast as my chair would move. To quote Hamlet, again, "there are more things in heaven and earth, Horatio, than are dreamt of in your philosophy."

To this day, I have no explanation of how I got out of there or who helped me. Was it a ghost, was it an angel, or was it a man? If it was a man what happened to him? Where did he come from and where did he go? Later, after I had time to think things over, there was one crazy thought that might explain things—that maybe my brother Jason was looking out for me. After that, I no longer went to the cemetery alone. I felt that I had no need to go back there.

Chapter Twenty-nine

Things I know

Don't take me for a fool.

Don't think of me as retarded or slow.

Just because I am stuck in a wheelchair,

Doesn't mean that there are things that I don't know.

I have walked in the sun,

And I have walked in the rain.

I have learned the hard lessons of life

Through countless sorrows and endless pain.

I have suffered and I have died.

I have passed through hell,

And come out the other side.

So if we should happen to meet

At the store or on the street,

Don't patronize me or treat me like a child.

Don't ignore me or think that I'm stupid.

That would be a waste of my time.

If you take the time to listen,

You might learn something.

You may be surprised.

You will find out that there are many things that I know.

I am actually fairly wise. The home care agency that Deann and I switched to was named Capstone. I thought it would be an improvement over Bannertrust, and at first it was. A couple of the aides went over with us as well. Even though Deann was no longer living with me, we still had to share some of the same aides and she started to pull the same shit again—telling the office that she didn't want this or that aide because she said they made her feel uncomfortable. So this meant that I wasn't able to have those aides to help me since we were both on the same shift. I finally got tired of it and I talked to the scheduler and had her taken off my shift. This made her mad to have that little bit of control over me taken away, but she found other ways to be a pain.

There were only two ways you could get into the apartment building. One was through the side door that opened with a key, and the other was through the main entrance, which used an intercom system or an electronic key card that all of the residents of the building were issued. Now most of the residents were smart enough not to loan out their keys. This meant an aide would have to call a person's room to be buzzed in or let into the building. I was not able to get out of bed by myself to answer the phone to let my aide into the building in the morning, so they would call Deann to let them in. But when she realized that the aide was for me, she would not answer her phone. This meant the aide had to call other apartments to be let in. Some of the people would get angry for being bothered or woken up, and they would complain. So after thinking about it for a few days, I came up with a simple solution to the problem of opening the door. I bought an inexpensive answering machine and hooked it up through my phone line.

I had learned from my boss Jack Vooge a little about pay phones and some of the devices that people use to fool them. They would sometimes use a recording of the different button tones to receive free calls. I had determined that the tone or sound of the button being pushed would open the door. A person didn't have to physically push the button at all to open the door, just as long as the intercom registered the correct tone. In this way I was able to trick the intercom into opening the door automatically when someone dialed my room through the lobby intercom.

There were other things that I had to figure out how to do now that I was living alone. One of these was how to get out of my front door. If I maneuvered my chair sideways close to the door I was able, with practice, to hook a few of my fingers through the door handle. Then putting my chair in reverse, I would back up slowly while simultaneously pressing down on the door handle, and the latch would pop open. I would back up until I hit the wall or until my fingers slipped off the handle. Then I would hurry around to get my foot petals wedged in the opening before the door shut. I was always too slow. The door had powerful spring hinges that would close the door shut the minute I let go of the handle. I needed a way around the problem, so I had the maintenance man disable my door. He loosened the hinges so I could now get out of my apartment by myself.

But it turned out that getting out the door was only half the problem, I now had to figure out a way of getting back in. The solution to this problem turned out to be surprisingly simple once I used my head to think about it. I mean I literally used my head to open the door. The door opened inwards, so my fingers would not work if I tried to hook them through the door handle—they would pull the door shut instead. So what I did was I would maneuver my chair out in the hall alongside my door, then lean over getting my head wedged under the handle and then lift up, popping the latch open. I would then add pressure to the door using my foot pedals to keep the door open. Then I would push through the open door and into my apartment.

Another thing I had to figure out was how to turn on my TV by myself. I managed this by attaching a piece of sticky Velcro to the back of my TV remote, and another piece to my night stand. Then backing my chair up to my night stand I was able to lean over and turn on the remote with my tongue. Most remotes have different shaped buttons for the volume, channel up, down, etc.: I was able to memorize the position of these buttons with ease. I hated having to depend on people for everything, so I tried to do as much stuff for myself as possible.

Being disabled and confined to a wheelchair is not easy for anyone. I would not wish such a fate on my worst enemy. With that said, I would like to address some of the fears and prejudices that are sometimes directed at disabled people. First, do not assume every person in a wheelchair is retarded or suffering from a learning disability; do not patronize or talk down to them like a child. It is rude and it tends to piss people off. A majority of physically disabled people are just ordinary healthy people same as you or I, but due to illness or injury are now disabled. Being placed in a wheelchair did not suddenly render them stupid, if anything it made them smarter. Hopefully they will learn the same important life lesson that my accident taught me, which is to take nothing for granted for it all can be taken away or lost in the blink of an eye. One of the most brilliant astrophysicists in the world, Steven Hawking, is in a wheelchair. What I am trying to say is don't judge a book by its cover. Second, being disabled is not a contagious disease. People fear what is not ordinary. Many times I have had little kids come up to me in a store. They were not afraid, they were curious. They wanted to know what happened to me, why I was in the wheelchair, and how I made it move. I guess to them my chair looked like a pretty neat toy. But nine times out of ten before one of my aides or I had a chance to explain anything to the child, a frightened mother would angrily whisk her child away, as if I were some kind of monster. What kind of message does that send to that child?

Chapter Thirty

I Stand

I stand upon the cliff,

Surveying the future

And reflecting on the past.

It's a long way down.

To jump would be so easy,

It would be so quick and so fast.

But I don't want to throw my life away,

Life isn't meant to be easy.

It's full of obstacles

In your way.

Problems will arise,

And they will pass.

Life is hard for a reason.

If it were easy,

We would all be damned. I wanted to do something with my life. I did not want to be stuck in my stupid apartment all the time. I wanted to go to college, but I wasn't sure how to go about it or where to start. I called the college in Brainerd, which was called Central Lakes Community College (CLC), to see what all I needed to apply. They told me that I would first need to submit a copy of my high school transcripts and also take a placement test to see if I could even be accepted.

I received my transcripts in the mail; they made for some interesting reading. I was a little disappointed to find that after twelve years of school I only ended up with a 2.8 grade point average. I thought for sure I had done better than that. Then I realized that none of the teachers were able to grade any of my tests for the last few months of my senior year because I was in the hospital. Most of them just gave me a C which was all right I guess. I did get one bad grade: a D minus in advanced algebra. To this day I still haven't used it, Mr. Rib! After receiving my transcripts, I set up an appointment to take the placement test.

When I was in high school I did not get around to taking my SATs, so I wasn't sure if that was the reason for the placement test, or if it was something that was required of all new students. Anyway, I did pretty awful on that stupid test. I think I may even have failed it if that was even possible. It wasn't that the test was stupid; there was just no easy way for someone like me to take it. I could not see to read any of the questions, nor was I able to use my hands to write down any of the answers. The people at the college didn't know what to do either. Finally they just recorded the test questions onto a tape recorder and had one of the students administer the test to me. I don't now but I think they could have thought of a better way, like reading it to me for instance. Like I said I had to listen to the test on tape, which was often hard to understand. I had to rewind and listen to parts more than once, which got confusing. I also had to help my test giver pronounce some of the words on her answer key, because she did not know how to say them.

After getting the results of the test, I was a little pissed off when the advisor suggested that I take a remedial English class, since that was what I had chosen for my major. I refused. I told her that I had already picked out a class that I wanted to take; it was Composition I, which was a writing course. I actually wanted to take creative writing but I had to take a prerequisite such as Comp I first.

I knew that trying to go back to school would be hard for me, but I wanted to prove to myself that I could do it. There was another reason: I needed something to occupy my time. I was growing very bored sitting around my apartment. I knew if I was given the chance, I could figure out a way to go to college, so that's what I did. The advisor agreed to let me sign up for the Composition class, which was my only class that semester. That's all I thought I could handle because it took me so long to write anything. I learned that I was not eligible for financial aid: they told me that I would have to take a minimum of two classes or so many credit hours to be eligible for financial aid. I am sure that I could have received possibly some kind of assistance for being a disabled student, but I chose to pay my own way. I didn't want to owe anyone, and it was important to me to do this on my own. So I saved my money for two months, which is hard to do when you are living on a fixed income. Finally, when I had enough saved, I wrote a check for my tuition, books, and all the miscellaneous crap like parking fees, etc. It came to a little over four hundred dollars. I was now an official registered college student and had the empty checking account to prove it.

Some people may take the opportunity to receive an education for granted, especially if someone else is footing the bill for you. In my opinion that is a stupid and irresponsible thing to do. There are many people who never have the opportunity or means to go to college. I think that getting an education is one of the most important things one can do for him or herself, but some of the most important lessons to be learned cannot be found in the classroom or in any book. They are life experiences that we all go through, they are life lessons. What you choose to learn from them is up to you.

Growing up in Minnesota, I now realize how fortunate I was to be able to attend decent public schools: the two-room schoolhouse where I went to kindergarten in Garrison, Minnesota, and the grade schools, middle school, junior high, and high school in Brainerd. The prospect of me starting college made me appreciate the free education that I received growing up.

Some people might wonder "what's so hard about taking one class per semester." At that rate I should have had a degree in about 20 years or so. But you have to remember, I had to invent a way to write, and the method was painstakingly slow to use at first. It has taken me nearly two years to make it this far on this book. For I have written nearly all of it by typing in Morse code with my tongue. I read somewhere that the tongue was the strongest muscle for its size in the human body. I have given mine a workout over the years. For instance, in order to type a simple word like work, I have to press a total of sixteen key clicks with my tongue. That can be a lot of slow *work*. But fortunately over the years, with practice, my typing speed has increased.

I was going to attempt to use my Virtual Morse program to go back to school. I didn't think anyone had ever tried doing homework by typing Morse code with one's tongue, but I was going to give it a shot. I had one of my home health aides go to class with me to take notes, then I would return home to type up my assignments on my computer. I had turned Deann's room into my office and computer room. I bought a computer desk but had to remove the drawers underneath so my knees would fit. Then I laid a thick sheet of Plexiglas over top the desk to make a smooth work area. That was my first makeshift writing studio. At first the writing was hard and I made a lot of mistakes. I needed to learn how to write properly. Any fool can write, I was proof of that, but to write properly or well was going to take some practice, as I would find out.

One of the things that the teacher had us do in class was to read over other students' papers and make corrections. We were to be honest and critique each other's papers. When I got my paper back, I was embarrassed and a bit angry at first. The kid who had my paper had been ruthless on a quest to find any little mistake. My paper was nearly covered in red check marks. It turned out that's exactly what I needed: someone to knock me down a few pegs and tell me what I was doing wrong. That kid did me a favor in pointing out my mistakes, such as sentence fragments, which I had a lot of. After that, I bought a program for my computer called Microsoft Word. It contained tools to help one's writing, such as spell check and grammar check, which helped me cut way down on my mistakes.

Since my Virtual Morse program was homemade and untested by anyone except me, I had to deal with any bugs that would pop up in the program. My brother Jack did his best to eliminate most of them, slowly improving the program in the process. But there was one problem in this early version that frustrated me and slowed me down a lot. Sometimes the words would get cut off the end of one or two of the sentences on the page when printed. I would have to try to remember what I had written and have someone write in the missing words later.

It was a pain, not to mention very time-consuming. But I kept at it, eventually receiving an A minus in the class.

The following year I signed up for another class: creative writing. I would have to wait until the fall semester when it would be offered. I missed the deadline for the winter semester and I looked at the spring and summer classes but I didn't see anything that interested me. So I had to wait until fall rolled around before I was able to sign up for it. Once again, I saved my money and paid for my tuition and books by myself. I had to buy a lot more books for this class, and I soon found out what a racket the bookstore can be. If you were lucky you may be able to find a used textbook that would have its price slightly reduced. But more often than not you will be forced to pay a princely sum for brand-spanking-new textbooks. At the end of the school year, if you want to try to sell your books back to the bookstore for some extra money, you might as well forget about it. For they will only pay you a tiny fraction of what you paid for them. I guess that's how they make their money.

The creative writing class was a bit more fun but also a lot more work. I had to do a lot more writing for this class. In addition to my daily assignments, I was to write four short stories, a brief autobiography, and an outline of a story of our choosing. This was to be accompanied by a query letter and a minimum of three thousand words for the story. So I set to work. I would write and do homework for six days a week, only taking a break on Sundays to watch the Minnesota Vikings football games. It still took me a very long time to write; it was excruciatingly slow work. For my final paper, the story I wrote about was of a fat guy who gets stranded in the woods in the middle of the winter when the snowmobile he is riding runs out of gas. Things soon turn from bad to worse as problems start to multiply for him. I wrote a twisted surprise-ending to it. It turned out to be over three thousand words and ten pages long. I added it up, and those ten pages for that story took me about one hundred hours to write. I ended up receiving an A in that class. Being able to complete those two college classes also brought my grade point average up to a 4.0.

Chapter Thirty-one

Eagle Eyes

Soaring to the heavens

So majestic, so high.

Circling slowly, on invisible currents of air.

Surveying the world below, with eagle eyes.

From mountain aerie, to lofty perch,

Through blinding sunlight, to the dark of clouds,

The piercing gaze of the eagle eye sees all.

Over meadows green, and forest old.

Down countless long years, untold.

I once saw the eagle eyes

As they flew over my head.

Our eyes connected,

And in that brief moment we could see into each other's souls.

Growing up in northern Minnesota, I learned to fish and hunt at a young age, mostly in the lakes and woods in and around my home. I loved the outdoors spending countless hours on the water, or walking through the frosty autumn woods bursting with brilliant fall colors, or exploring a frozen, snow-covered tamarack swamp on snowshoes. I felt like the woods and water were a part of me, as if it were somehow in my blood. The memories of those times would sustain me through the painful dark months and years ahead.

One memory in particular would calm me during the worst of my hellish pain and agony, lying in my hospital bed, racked by seizures and muscle spasms, and soaked in sweat. Delirious with pain and fever as my withered body writhed in pain from the unseen tormentors, I would pray for death and for the endless sleep to end this hellish nightmare. In the midst of my agony, when I thought I could not endure another moment of pain, I would think about the eagle and it would help calm me. I used this memory sparingly, like a powerful drug. It became part of my private medicine chest.

The summer before my accident when I was seventeen, I woke early one morning, well before sunrise. I lay there in my dark room listening to the loons cry out on the lake behind the house. Their mournful cries drifted up to me through my open window, making me shiver involuntarily with goose bumps. If you have ever heard the loons cry in the stillness of a fog-shrouded dawn you will understand.

Unable to go back to sleep, and not having to go to work that day, I decided to go for a paddle. So after throwing on some clothes and slipping into my moccasins, I headed down the dew-covered lawn to retrieve my kayak from the sandy shore of the lake. It was made of fiberglass, and measured a little over thirteen feet long and weighed about forty pounds. Picking it up with one hand, I carried it back over the lawn to my waiting car, then with one fluid motion I would heave the boat onto the roof of my car and precede to tie it down.

Then, taking my paddle from the garage, I set out for the big lake. It was about three miles to Lake Mille Lacs where I planned to watch the sunrise and spend the day paddling. After unloading my boat near the mouth of a small creek, I let the current carry me out into the lake. I gave a few strokes of my paddle, gliding soundlessly through the ragged curtains of mist that lay atop the dark water. I loved the peaceful stillness of this hour, where I was alone on the lake.

Stretching out to the horizon before me lay the still dark waters of Lake Mille Lacs, nearly one hundred miles around and one of the largest in the state. I sat there motionless, floating lightly upon the water with my gaze fixed on the eastern horizon. Soon, a rosy blush began to appear in the eastern sky. I waited patiently as the darkness started to recede and the day slowly brightened. Soon, the first blinding rays of the sunshine pierced the far horizon, and like some giant fiery beast, the sun slowly rose into the sky. I did not know it at the time that this would be my last sunrise that I would ever watch over the lake.

For some reason, I never made it back there again to watch the sunrise. I was preoccupied with other things I guess by that time, work, school, girls, and the typical life of a teenager. Not knowing that in a few short months I would be dead. I wish now that I would have taken the time to appreciate a few more sunrises.

Turning southeast I began paddling, following the shoreline about a hundred yards out in the lake. After about five or six miles, I came to a sandy stretch of shoreline that was known locally as Carlsona Beach. Perched atop the highest, most branches of a dead elm that rose a hundred feet above the water sat an enormous bald eagle. Apparently it had been watching me for some time. I stopped paddling and just sat still, laying my paddle down across my boat. I don't know how long I sat there gazing up at the eagle, with our eyes on one another. It suddenly lifted into the air, and in one graceful, sweeping motion, it glided down over the water, heading directly for me.

I sat frozen, feeling strangely hypnotized by the sight of the onrushing bird. As it drew closer, I remained still; I was helpless to do anything else but watch. There was a sudden roar and rush of wind as the eagle streaked by, three feet above my head. But for the briefest of moments when the eagle was directly overhead our eyes locked and I saw something I cannot explain. It then veered to the right, sailing effortlessly over the water about two hundred yards from shore. I watched as it calmly brushed the surface of the water with one of its talons and then returned to its perch on the tree with a fish in his claws. That eagle had just shown me who was boss of the lake, and with that I turned around and headed back the way I came. I spent the rest of the day paddling and thinking about the eagle. It was these kinds of memories that I would call upon during my months of darkness and pain.

The outdoors have always been a big part of my life, but now that I am disabled, there are many things that I miss doing. But I have been able to teach a few what I knew.

When I lived in Brainerd, my family would visit from Ohio twice a year, once in the summer and again over Christmas. My dad, brother, and I always made it a point to try to do some fishing on these visits. During the summer we would rent a fishing launch or pontoon boat to go fishing, or to cruise around the different lakes. In the winter when the lakes would freeze over, we would go ice fishing, sometimes loading my chair on a sled to pull me through the snow to the fish house.

There are two different types of ice fishing: angling, and dark house spear fishing. For angling, you would drill multiple holes in the ice that you would lower your hook, line and bobber into. For dark house spear fishing, you cut a large hole in the ice, maneuvering a windowless open floored fish house over the hole. Suspended from the ceiling directly over the hole is a fishing reel that holds a line that can be lowered into the water, often attached to this is a large live minnow, or a weighted wooden decoy. A person would sit on a seat next to the hole with a metal spear that is attached to their wrist by a length of thin rope or cord. Then when a fish appears in the hole to go after the bait, the person throws the spear like a harpoon, in an attempt to impale a fish on the spear. My dad built a wheelchair accessible spear house so I was able to go along ice fishing.

During the summer I tried to go back to the lake where I grew up as much as possible to sit and listen to the waves, or to watch the sunset and smell the clean fresh scent of the lake. I had taught one of my aides how to fish and another how to clean fish. Years later, I would also teach five people how to bow hunt, with each of them shooting and killing deer in the process.

Chapter Thirty-two

Cash Cow

So high, in the noonday sky

The vultures circle, far and wide.

Riding upon the thermals of air,

Their slow orbits, casting shadows of death across the peaceful day,

Searching for any sign of weakness, death or decay.

The vultures, they follow me wherever I go.

Greedily they follow me around.

I am watched-over night and day.

To them, I am a wounded cash cow.

And like the scavengers they are,

They feed upon my guts.

Ravenously gorging themselves

And lining their pockets with my misery.

Home care agencies are only as good as the quality of the people they hire. Capstone was no exception. I think some of the agencies start out with good intentions of wanting to help people, but what invariably happens is they get greedy when they see how much money there is to be made in the healthcare business. When a home care agency or nursing home can receive hundreds of dollars per day for one single client, more often than not they will try to take on more and more clients to increase their profits. This results in a loss of focus on the part of the agency to provide quality patient care to their clients. They often lose track of their priorities, putting profits ahead of their clients and employees. What they often fail to realize is that if it weren't for the clients and the aides who care for them, the home care companies would not be in business.

I switched to Capstone home health care agency because I thought it would be an improvement, and because they were one of the few agencies that would allow their aides to drive me in my van. I am not exactly sure what kind of standards or guidelines, if any, home care agencies have to follow when hiring their employees. The thing about Capstone that I found to be disturbing and a bit frightening at times was that they would hire anyone.

They would take a stranger off the street with no training or experience and send him or her into your home to care for you. Needless to say, there were some problems. There were incidents where an aide's background check failed to clear, but the aide had been hired and been working before anything was discovered. They hired people who could barely read; they hired one girl who suffered from multiple personalities and violent mood swings. There was another girl that Capstone hired who would go dumpster diving for food and think nothing of it. It was sad, but when she tried to eat out of my trash can that was too much. I had to tell her no.

These were just a few examples of the kinds of people that Capstone hired to care for me. I did have a few good aides for awhile, but as so often is the case most of them ended up leaving, either to get married, or to move on to better paying jobs. Though the owners of a home care agency may take in thousands of dollars in one day, they will often only pay their employees a pittance of the profits. Most places will only hire home health aides part-time so they can avoid paying overtime and insurance benefits. That is one of the reasons why there is such a high turnover rate in the home care industry. I am not trying to discourage anyone from entering the health care field, particularly home care, God knows good help is hard to find. There is a need for nurses and home health aides to care for people in their homes. Accidents happen, people get sick, and eventually everyone will get old someday. If you enjoy helping and caring for others, then home care may be a job that would interest you, but if all you are interested in is a paycheck, I don't think that home health care is the right job for you.

There are alternatives to home care agencies; one of these is called the independent provider care option, or IP. This program pays a bit more than a home care agency and employees are paid by the state, as opposed to an agency. Since Capstone would hire just about anyone, some of the aides they hired turned out to be dishonest. I would discover cash missing from my wallet from time to time, along with other things like my pills, and even beer from my refrigerator. Each time it would happen I would notify the Capstone office of the theft, in the hope that something could be done, but nothing ever was. This was very disappointing and upsetting to me.

These people were hired to care for me, and I had to depend on them and trust them. I hated feeling so helpless and vulnerable. How was I expected to depend on and trust people when people they hired were not dependable or trustworthy? I didn't know what to do or who to turn to for help. The office would not listen to me; instead they told me that it was my own fault that people were stealing from me. I failed to see the logic in that statement. That really upset me. Things were going downhill. I got to the point where I didn't trust anybody anymore, including Deann. I felt like everyone had turned against me—I felt trapped and a bit paranoid. I needed help, but I could not trust the people who were hired to help me. I started making plans to leave Capstone, but trying to keep a secret in an apartment building is pretty much next to impossible. I informed one person who was the scheduler and to her credit she kept her word and didn't tell anyone of my plans, not even the owner of the company. This made the owner mad when she eventually found out, but by that time there was not much more she could do about it. She did manage to inflict one parting shot. I didn't know if it was out of spite or what, but when she found out what date I was planning on leaving, she deliberately set my last day of service one week short of the day I planned to leave. It turned out to be a blessing in disguise, though it was a bit of an inconvenience for my dad. But as for me, I was more than happy to leave that place a week early.

Chapter Thirty-three

My Minnesota

I have stood upon the high barren cliffs to watch the sunrise break over the most superior of all ten thousand lakes. This is my Minnesota.

I have walked across the start of the Mississippi river, where it is born from the algae-covered rocks. This is my Minnesota.

I have stood in the deep portage where the voyagers rested before pushing on. Into the boundary waters to the lands beyond. This is my Minnesota.

I have hiked and climbed in the stone quarries at Sandstone, and I have swum in the deep iron pits of Cuyuna, where the waters are always icy cold. This is my Minnesota.

I have seen the prairie winds blow through a sea of wild flowers and buffalo grass, stretching to the horizon like an endless green sea. This is my Minnesota.

I have walked on water, and I have lived among the saints, such as Paul, Joseph, and Saint Cloud. This is my Minnesota.

I have walked through a virgin forest untouched by the hand of man, and I have been to the sister cities full of noise and traffic jams. This is my Minnesota.

I have gazed upon the Gooseberry, Taylor, and Minnehaha Falls. And I have slept in the blue earth before the foot of cliff walls. This is my Minnesota.

I hold these memories close to my heart they are part of me, when I travel afar. This is my Minnesota.When my brother Jason died, my parents gave away many of his things. I believe my mom donated his clothes to the Goodwill along with a set of golf clubs to one of the schools. At the time of his death, he also had five hundred dollars in his billfold. This my mom tearfully passed on to her five remaining children. We each ended up receiving a one hundred dollar bill. At first I didn't want to accept it, being very upset at the time. My mom told me that my brother would want me to have the money. I had no doubt that she was probably right, so I took the money but I could not bring myself to spend it. Instead, I used the hundred dollars to open a savings account, which over the next several years I added to every chance I got, in preparation and hopes that I might have a chance to move someday.

My parents were living in Ohio at the time. I would keep in touch with them by e-mail and by phone, though it was often hard for them to understand me over the phone at times. I had told them a little of what had been happening, holding most everything else back not wanting to worry or upset them. They wanted me to move to Ohio to be closer to them, but I didn't want to give up my independence nor did I want to be a burden on them. Minnesota was my home. I didn't want to leave; it was all I knew. But in truth, I was afraid of change, but I soon realized no matter how hard you try to keep everything the same, nothing lasts forever and nothing can remain unchanged. So after the third straight month of being ripped off by my home health aides and being told that it was my fault by the owner of the home care agency, I finally agreed to move to Ohio.

So over the course of the next ten months, working mostly nights and weekends, my dad and brothers along with friends and neighbors of my parents all helped to build me my own house. That was about the nicest thing that anyone has ever done for me. I was able to give my dad input on the floor plan so he could design the house to be as wheelchair accessible as possible. In the meantime, I would have to be patient and wait for the construction to be finished before I could move into the house. I had mixed feelings about moving to Ohio. On one hand I was nervous and excited with the thought of living a thousand miles away and also with the thought of having my own place. On the other hand, I had the feeling that I had somehow sold out, allowing myself to be pushed away from all of the places I once loved. But in the end I said my good-byes and moved.It is amazing the amount of stuff that one person can accumulate over the years. I had been living in Brainerd for several years, and when I moved I was surprised at the amount of stuff I had. I gave a lot of it away to my friends, things like winter clothing and fishing gear, plus four or five brown grocery bags full of shoes and clothes that I gave to the Goodwill. But I still found that I had too much stuff. I ended up leaving behind a sofa, an air conditioner, and some other stuff that would not fit in the moving trailer. When it was all said and done, I had the moving trailer packed to the gills with my stuff. I had three wheelchairs, two of which were power chairs, along with a manual pushchair and also a wheeled shower chair that I crammed in as well. Last but not least, I packed up my bed barely managing to squeeze it into the trailer. I don't care who you are, moving is always a pain in the ass. After turning in my keys to my apartment, I set off for my new home in Ohio.

Chapter Thirty-four

The Old Man

The old man.

There is an old man who lives in the forest.

He has been there for as long as anyone can remember.

His skin harbors deep grooves and the scars of old age.

He is a very old man.

He is a kindly grandfather of a man.

He spends his time feeding the squirrels and the deer.

He even makes birdhouses from time to time.

He is a generous old man.

He is not greedy or materialistic.

He has no use for money.

He is content to live off the land.

He is a simple old man.

He has lived his whole life in one place.

In the place of his birth,

Same as his mother and father before him.

With his roots set, he has not ventured far.

But his children and his children's children,

Continue to scatter further and further away.

Last week they killed the old man.

They murdered him in his sleep

As he dozed in the afternoon sun.

As the first chainsaw bit into his side,

He cried out in agony.

The men did not listen,

Nor did they hear.

The squirrels stared and the deer were silent

As they watched the old man fall to earth.

The old man that used to feed the squirrels and deer,

The old man who made birdhouses from time to time,

Was dead.

Murdered while he slept in the afternoon sun.

Sometime later I went back to pay my respects to the old man.

As I sat on his stump,

I started to count the rings.

When I got to two hundred, I stopped.

I felt like crying.

How could something so majestic, so magnificent, and so grand—

How could it be lost forever?

In a matter of minutes.

September 10, 2002

Moving to Ohio was like entering another country, one with a foreign landscape and customs. Gone were the clear cool lakes of Minnesota to be replaced by hills and valleys thickly forested with all manner of hardwood trees. This was coalmine country, full of steep hills and deep shady ravines. Throughout the state were hundreds of abandoned mine shafts and strip pits. Many of the open pits are now flooded and now are stocked with pan fish where the coal was once dug from the ground.

My house was situated on the side of a hill surrounded by trees, overlooking a dirt road and a small stream that was known as Peters Creek, which snaked its way along the valley bottom between two steep hills. I was now living in the country. It was very peaceful, and for the most part, the neighbors were few but also pretty nice. It was a hundred times quieter than living in my apartment in Brainerd, where all I heard was the constant noise of traffic from semis, ambulances, and the steady line of cars that visited a drug house down the block—their horns honking all hours of the night. Now all I hear in the evenings are the buzz and whine of cicadas and crickets, along with the deep rubber band twang sound of the bullfrogs. Occasionally you will hear the low echoing hoot of a great horned owl, or the shrill plaintive cries of coyotes; that is all.

Moving to Ohio was a bit of a culture shock for me and took some getting used to. For the first month or so I had a hard time figuring out what the people who lived here were saying. Their expressions, phrases, and colloquialisms were all very strange and different to my ears. There were times when I questioned myself if what I was hearing was even English and not some kind of redneck language. But I was somewhat relieved to find that my parents and brothers all reported similar thoughts upon first moving to Ohio.

It was sort of a different culture. Here many things were different. For instance, I was a little surprised at the number of drive-thru liquor stores and carry out places that some towns have. People were able to place an order and buy beer without even getting out of their cars. This was very different from the towns where I lived in Minnesota. There were also dry towns in Ohio, where the sale of alcohol is prohibited. It's as if prohibition was never repealed. I thought that was rather interesting. One disturbing aspect of living here was an undercurrent of prejudice and racism that seemed to surround some people and communities. I personally found it to be very distasteful and ugly. I don't know if I was sheltered or just naive, but they still have the KKK here. I thought that was pretty messed up. The scary part is that these people pass on their beliefs to their children, no matter how misguided or messed up those beliefs may be. I have met people here who were sweet as could be, and good-looking and attractive, but some of the racial comments and garbage I heard spew from their mouths made them very ugly. I have said it before: do not judge a book by its cover. Sometimes beautiful people are ugly, and sometimes ugly people can be beautiful. It all depends on one's point of view.

Before moving to Ohio, I had my mom send me a phone book from the town that my parents were live in. I wanted it so I could sort of scope out the area and see what this town had to offer. Another reason I wanted the phone book was so I could write to the home care agencies in the area and do my best to check them out beforehand. This I did by sending out close to a dozen letters to different home care agencies. Not all of them answered me, but quite a few of them did. From their replies, I was able to narrow my search and pick what I hoped to be a good company.

Though every home care agency has its share of problems from time to time, I had done my research and picked the one I thought had the most going for it. Number one, they were nationally known. This meant they had a web site that I was able to go to to find information. Also, the local office was computerized so I could reach them by e-mail if I had a question or problem. This was a plus for me, since I was not easily able to dial a telephone. Some home care agencies do not own a computer. Second, this company trained its employees, sending out new aides with veteran aides to show them the ropes making sure the new aide is competent and comfortable with the job. This is important;

not all agencies train their help. I have been dropped and hurt by aides who were not trained and didn't know what they were doing. Third, this company allowed its employees to drive me in my van. This was also a plus, for it provided me with some mobility and independence, which is very important to me.

Living in Ohio was okay, but also boring at times. I did not have a job to go to or a girlfriend to spend time with. I needed something to do to keep from going stir crazy. I had planned on going back to school, but those plans didn't turn out how I had hoped. I applied twice to two colleges in the area. I had paid my registration fee both times, and both times the home health care aide that I had lined up to take me ended up going elsewhere. By this time it was too late to find someone else, so I was not able to go. The thing about home health is that there is a very high turnover rate. It is true that some people think that the grass is always greener somewhere else. This is true for home health aides as well. Trying to find steady, reliable help can sometimes be hard to come by.

Chapter Thirty-five

A Walk in the Woods

I miss the simple pleasure of walking in the woods.

The leaves under my feet, the smell of the air so fresh and sweet.

No barking dogs, no sirens wail, only peace and quiet fill the air.

I miss the mossy rocks, the ferns so green, and the sticky sap from the

evergreens.

I walked slowly with measured steps, inspecting the grass where deer

once slept.

I miss the rustle of the leaves, and the way the sun peeks through the

canopy.

Yes, I miss the simple pleasure of walking in the woods. I wanted to do so much but was not physically able to do so. This was very frustrating for me. Though I had learned out of necessity to do many things in different ways, there were still a lot of things I miss doing, like fishing and hunting. Ohio has very few lakes and none of them happen to be close to my house. But what Ohio did have was lots and lots of deer. They were a very common sight in the farmer's fields, and also in the grassy roadside ditches. I often have them very near to my house, ten yards or less.

I began thinking of ways I could hunt or, to be more precise, ways I could teach someone to hunt for me. Though I was not able to see or pull the trigger, I was able to teach someone to hunt and in turn they became my eyes and hands. My first hunting pupil was one of my home health aides. She was a very petite, small girl standing four feet ten inches tall, and maybe ninety pounds soaking wet. She had shot a deer before with a gun, but ever since my brother died people with guns have made me nervous. I have always preferred using a bow and arrow to hunt, as opposed to a gun. It was quieter, and with only one shot it made for more of a challenge and also less chance of an accident.

I was going to attempt to teach her how to shoot a bow. This was no easy task since most bows were either too big or too powerful for her to pull back with her short, little arms. I finally went to an archery shop and had them special order the smallest crossbow that they carried.

In Ohio, you are allowed to use crossbows to hunt. Also, I thought it would be easier for her to learn, since it was similar to shooting a gun. I believe the crossbow had a draw weight of about seventy-five pounds. This was the force it took to pull the string back and cock the bow. The force needed was also reduced by two pulleys that were attached to the bow, which made it easier to pull the string back to cock the bow, and also increased the arrow's speed. Even so, it was still too hard for her to cock the bow with her short little arms and legs.

I had to purchase a mechanical device to help her pull the bowstring back. I taught her which way to place the arrow, how to use the safety, how to look through the sights, and how to aim. With practice she became a very good shot. After my accident, I thought my hunting days were over. It wasn't until moving to Ohio (of all places) that I was given the chance to hunt once again.

One day while talking with my dad, I mentioned an idea I had for a wheelchair accessible deer stand. I went on to explain about the ramp platform that I once saw at an archery range. He thought it was a good idea. So after clearing a path, he built the stand in the woods behind my house, covering the sides with camouflage and brush. Soon bow season was open and with his crossbow in hand, I followed my dad up the ramp and into the stand.

It didn't bother me that I was unable to shoot. For me, hunting wasn't so much about always shooting animals as it was just enjoying the outdoors, listening to the music of the birds, watching the squirrels and chipmunks scamper about, and just breathing in the rich, sweet, earthy smell of the woods. As I sat there, the sun began to sink behind the hills, turning the treetops golden in the fading light. The crickets started to sing, which was followed by the peeping chorus of the tree frogs. Then, like some trick of shadow and light everything seemed to stand still as if the trees were holding their breath. And in that moment three deer stepped out from the tree line, appearing without a sound, like magic.

Over the next couple of years I would teach five of my home health aides how to bow hunt, with each of them successfully harvesting deer. My friends and family have taken over twenty-five deer from my tree stand the few years I have had it. Some of you reading this may be non-hunters, or against hunting all together; we hunt for the venison. I don't expect you to understand how someone could kill and eat such a fuzzy cute animal, right? But the fact is that deer meat or venison is delicious. And the next time you total your car spending thousands on repairs from hitting a deer; it may change your thinking about the role hunter's play.

Chapter Thirty-six

Island

I have been stuck on this island for a very long time.

Cut off from the world, with nowhere to go and nowhere to hide.

I sit here, imprisoned by the water that surrounds me from all sides.

I have no boat, and no raft.

With no hope of rescue and no way to get back.

Back to the life I left behind,

The people and places that I knew so well, at one time.

But you cannot live in the past, feeling sorry for yourself,

Thinking how different your life could have been.

Sometimes you just have to make up your mind and swim. Like I said, living in Ohio could be boring and also lonely at times. I really didn't know anybody. The only people I really saw apart from my parents were my home health aides. I have had relationships with some of my aides in the past, but nothing too serious and nothing lasting. Most home care companies have rules against such things. With nothing to do all day, feeling frustrated and bored I began doing the only thing I could think of to pass the time and to vent my frustrations and that was to write.

I began writing poems as a way to vent. I wrote about five hundred before I quit. I wrote a collection of humorous short stories about growing up in Minnesota, which made my family laugh. I also wrote some articles and short stories for a resort newsletter that my uncle's company put out. I wanted to try something different, so I took one of my poems and turned it into an illustrated children's book. I had a friend of my brother's draw the artwork for it. That was a learning experience for me. I tried unsuccessfully to get it published. In the end, I gave the remaining copies away to people who had kids.

About this time I met a guy named Craig Sticklemeyer. He was an outdoor writer for the local newspaper, and also happened to work for one of my uncle's resorts at the time. He was an avid bow hunter as well. My dad invited him over for dinner one night, and we talked about bow hunting and writing. I showed him some of my short stories and a copy of the children's book I wrote, also my Morse code switch for my computer. He was impressed. He asked me to write an article for the newspaper about my deer stand, so I did. It accompanied an article that he wrote about disabled sportsmen.

We've been hunting together many times ever since, with me acting as the hunting guide, my acute hearing pinpointing and warning him of deer long before he was able to spot them. Also razzing him when he happens to miss, like the time he shot two trees with his bow in one night. Since Craig worked at the newspaper, I was able to meet one of his colleagues. He was a feature writer for the same paper. His name was John Lowe. He wrote a story about me and what had happened to me and also how I use Morse code to write. He sent me a list of questions and we were able to conduct an interview by e-mail. When his article about me appeared in the newspaper, I saw that my answers to his interview questions along with my statements and comments were left whole and unedited. This meant a lot to me, that he hadn't tried to change what I had said. My mom bought about twenty copies to send to friends and relatives.

I thanked John Lowe for writing the article; I had learned a lot from him. He was very helpful with answering questions pertaining to writing. He also helped me by giving me a name of a guy who did some copyediting. His name was John or Joe Baker, I don't remember. I had been searching for someone to help edit some of my poems and he agreed to help. He helped correct many of my mistakes also pointing out what I was doing wrong and making suggestions. John Lowe had told him what had happened to me and of my situation. He suggested that I should write a book about my life. I told him that I wasn't sure; I had always been a private person—besides, I didn't know anything about writing books. I had never written anything longer than a dozen or so pages in my life. To write a whole book seemed like a monumental task. I didn't know where to start, but he agreed to help. So I sent him a few chapters and he gave me some suggestions, and then I was on my own. I didn't know how to even go about it. I could not take notes. I would have to keep everything organized inside my head, which I knew would be very hard. The idea of a blind man writing a book was crazy. But if John Milton could write *Paradise Lost* while being completely blind, I thought to myself, *what was preventing me from writing a book as well?* For those of you who do not know who John Milton was, he was an English writer and poet who lived in the sixteenth century. After losing his eyesight he continued to write, publishing two books, *Paradise Lost* and *Paradise Found*. The big difference between the two of us was that he did not have to write with his tongue.

So after thinking it over, I decided to give it a try, and after three years of work, here is my story. Maybe it can help some people, perhaps to inspire them or hopefully open their eyes and see things from a different point of view. We all have successes and failures in our lives, along with hard choices and mistakes. To go back in time and know

now what you didn't know then. I think most of us would like the opportunity to make different choices. Too bad life does not work that way. I believe life is a test. And the lessons are sometimes very hard for a reason. What you choose to learn from your life is entirely up to you. I leave you with a quote from the book *The Adventures of Huckleberry Finn*, by the author and humorous Samuel Clemens: "So there isn't nothing more to write about and I am rotten glad of it because if I'd a known what a trouble it was to make a book I wouldn't a tackled it and ain't a going to do no more."

"The End"

CPSIA information can be obtained at www.ICGtesting.com
Printed in the USA
BVOW011604041212

307260BV00002B/212/P